Abandonment

Abandonment

"The Plague of Most Men"

Damon Jones

Noahs Ark Publishing
Beverly Hills, California

Abandonment: The Plague of Most Men

ISBN 978-0-578-76106-0

Copyright © 2020 by Damon Jones

Published by:

Noahs Ark Publishing Service
8549 Wilshire Blvd., Suite 1442
Beverly Hills, CA 90211

www.noahsarkpublishing.com

Editor: Rebekah J. Trout
Graphic Design: Theodore Wright IV
Interior Design: James Sparkman

I dedicate this book to these very special people in my life:

To my father, Austin Lee Jones

I forgive you, Dad, with no judgments. I love you.

To my son, Keenan L. Jones

My mission is to become the father you deserve, with the guidance and direction of God. Please, forgive me for not being there for you. Don't allow the cycle of abandonment and anger to continue because of my failures and absence in your life. My heart will always be open for you whenever you're ready to have a conversation. I love you, Son.

Contents

Acknowledgements

My best friend and amazing wife, Debra Jones
Without you, I wouldn't be the man I am today through Christ. Thank you for loving me, in spite of me. Your "Bear" will always love you for eternity. You're most definitely the angel God created just for me.

My mother, Lela Jones
Without your prayers, I would be dead or in prison. I can never thank you enough for never giving up on me. Thank you for being my greatest example of courage and perserverance. I love you, Mom.

My adopted grandmother, Mother Barbara Jean Henderson
Thank you opening your heart and being such a powerful woman of God. I'll always cherish our deep and thought-provoking conversatons. I love and miss you.

The father and mother of my queen, Robert and Susie Morris
Thank you for your valued and appreciated conversations of insight and wisdom. I love you.

The mother of my queen, Eddie Mae Morris White
Thank you for giving birth to my angel who was sent from Heaven just for me. I love you.

Pastor Kalvin & First Lady Pamela Kressel
Your godly counsel and wisdom are what kept me grounded when I accepted Jesus into my life. Thank you for being an amazing godly example. You'll always be my Pastor and First Lady. I love you.

Bonita Thomas
Thank you for being such a true woman of God. Keep pursuing your purpose with passion. Stay encouraged. I love you.

Rick Bengco
Thank you for being my younger brother from another mother. Stay encouraged. I love you.

Corey Walker
Thank you for having a genuine heart for God. You're wise beyond your age. God has an amazing plan for your life. Stay encouraged. I love you.

Kolo Goshi
Thank you for your heart-to-heart fellowship. Remain focused on your God-directed path. Stay encouraged. I love you.

Chris Slack
Thank you for being a genuine and sincere soldier of Christ. I truly appreciate your words of wisdom and inspiration. Stay encouraged. I love you.

Rod Johnson
Always remember that you're not on the battlefield alone. Thank you for being an authentic and sincere soldier of Christ. Stay encouraged. I love you.

Introduction

Surprise! Your father has died and you have six brothers and sisters you never knew you had. The year was 2004. I received a phone call from a woman in Texas informing me that my father had died—a man whom I had never met face-to-face, a man who was physically and verbally abusive to my mother, a man who never wanted anything to do with me, a man who didn't even want to speak with me on the phone when all I wanted was to hear his voice. The woman on the phone claimed to be my oldest sister, one of the sisters I had never known.

I never realized how angry I was about my father not being present in my life until she asked, "Are you coming to Daddy's funeral?" In my mind, I couldn't believe that she had the nerve to ask that question. All I could think was, "Daddy's funeral? He was never a so-called 'daddy' to me." My reply was a quick, "NO. I'm not coming," without hesitation or feeling. I didn't feel any emotion for this man, a man who was supposed to be my father, and I wasn't going to his funeral in Texas. All I felt was anger because he had left this earth without me being able to ask one simple question, "Why didn't you want to be part of my life?" I was deeply angry and I didn't truly know why!

Prior to that phone call, I had spent thirty-six years only aware of the older sister and brother whom I had grown up with. I never imagined that an old song would be the mental trigger for any thoughts I would have about my father. You know the song,

It was the third of September
That day I'll always remember, yes I will
'Cause that was the day that my daddy died
I never got a chance to see him
Never heard nothin' but bad things about him
Momma I'm depending on you to tell me the truth
Momma just hung her head and said,
"Son, PAPA WAS A ROLLING STONE,
wherever he laid his hat WAS HIS HOME
and WHEN HE DIED, all he left me was ALONE."

My father's death was the catalyst for my journey of forgiveness and transformation—from a male to a Kingdom man—through my trust and faith in Jesus Christ.

I take full responsibility for all of my choices in life; however, I've always wondered how my life would've turned out if my father had been an active part of it. I have nothing but the highest respect for my mother, but she couldn't fill the void left inside me from abandonment and feeling totally unwanted by my father. My non-existent relationship with my father was the main connection to why I unknowingly and instinctually continued the cycle with my own son. As of the writing of this book, the first communication between my son and me in nearly nine years occurred recently, through a text on his birthday. Until recently, and after fifty-one years of living, I didn't have true clarity about why my relationship with my son has been strained. Clarity came to me one day while brainstorming about this book with a man who had a similar background as mine—one without an active father in his life. After this conversation, I discovered that I had been judging my son because of my stubbornness and pride.

The principle lesson I'd like to share with you is this: I'm going to do whatever I can to reach my son. Wherever he is, I'll share my heart and take full responsibility for why I wasn't as active in his life as I could've been. I'm going to end the cycle that began with the absence of my father with intentional action, prayer, faith, and continually seeking God's guidance. Christ opened my eyes that most likely my father never had a Kingdom man's guidance in his life either, and that was why he didn't know how to be a caring father to me.

I felt the need to share my personal testimony in this book—with full transparency—to help any boys and men who might be struggling with the issues associated with abandonment. In *Abandonment*, I will share that God didn't cause the bullying I experienced as a child, but He allowed it, which led me to becoming an angry boy who grew into an angry male. I risked everything for attention!

My true writing inspiration came when I accepted Jesus Christ as my Lord and Savior on February 25, 2001. After that day, I began to have a strong feeling from within to share my story. I felt it needed to be shared with other men who think they have to fight this battle of life alone. My goal is to share my life story in the most transparent, open, and vulnerable way. I want to encourage other males from boyhood to their golden years to seek and become the men whom God created and intended them to be. It's NEVER TOO LATE!

CHAPTER ONE

He Didn't Cause It, but He Allowed It

"AND WE KNOW THAT GOD WORKS ALL THINGS TOGETHER FOR THE GOOD OF THOSE WHO LOVE HIM, WHO ARE CALLED ACCORDING TO HIS PURPOSE." (ROMANS 8:28 BSB)

I was born in Lubbock, Texas, but soon after my birth, my mother had to make a life-changing decision for the safety of herself and her three young children. After years of physical and verbal abuse from my father, my mother fled to California with her children in the 1970s. My mother's actions were truly courageous because she chose to leave a toxic and unhealthy situation and moved us to Los Angeles, with her trust and faith firmly in God. We arrived in a very unfamiliar and menacing place with only the clothes in our suitcases. We lived in various areas of Los Angeles, but my mother ultimately ended up purchasing a home in Compton.

From the earliest time I can remember, I had always been a shy and introverted child. I had no idea that would be the main cause of most of my childhood pain—which became very apparent when I entered elementary school. Simply put, kids can be very cruel. Just like any child, all I wanted was to be liked and accepted, but I was neither of these. At that young age, I didn't understand why I was being singled out by the other kids. They called me various names and wouldn't allow me to be part of any of their groups because I wasn't popular. As an adult, I now understand why the kids thought it was okay to ridicule me. Even though they knew it wasn't right to tease and bully me, many of them felt, "Better you than me."

As a child, many times the need to be accepted is more powerful than doing what's right, and what's right is often not popular. The teasing and bullying never escalated to being physical in nature; however, the psychological and mental damage that was done to me was far worse. Please don't get me wrong, I had some great experiences during elementary school, but unfortunately, the only ones that I truly remember are the painful ones. The teachers did what they could whenever they witnessed any of the teasing, but I believed that they could've—and should've—done more. The bullying continued on throughout the rest of my time in elementary, and through the ninth grade. Away from school, the bullying even included others stealing bicycles from me on numerous occasions.

This truly took a tremendous toll on my self-worth and self-confidence because the main focus of the cruelty was directed at the size of my head—something about me I had no control over. Through my tears, I began to accept the bullying and teasing as my new reality for the rest of my life. In junior high school it intensified, and to my surprise, someone came up with a new name for me inspired by the Disney character, Pinocchio. For those of you that aren't familiar with Pinocchio, it is the story of a wooden boy whose nose grows every time he doesn't tell the truth. Well, instead of Pinocchio, they called me "Pinocchi-Head," because they said that instead of my nose growing, my forehead would grow when I lied. On other occasions, kids would ask me, "Are you even black?" That would escalate to the kids calling me, "white boy." After years of bullying and teasing, I began to feel strong resentment, a lack of trust, and uneasiness growing within me towards people in general.

I didn't blame God, because I didn't have a relationship with God during my childhood. Like many people, I grew up in the church, but I didn't have a true understanding of God as a child. Even now, as a mature Christian man, I still don't blame God because I have more clarity about Him not *causing* the bullying, but *allowing* it. In my opinion, I truly believe that God allowed the bullying to condition me for the struggles of life and to be an effective witness. I know it sounds a bit odd, but I finally understand that God uses all situations, good or bad, for His purpose. Romans 8:28 states that everything works for our good, but it took me many years to even grasp a basic understanding of what that truly meant. In spite of the pain I felt throughout my childhood, I don't have any regrets about what I had to endure. I've found that pain has been instrumental in my life in many ways. I know that it pained God to put me through the hurt of the bullying and teasing in my childhood, but it was necessary to strengthen me for His purpose.

As a result of the teasing and bullying I endured, I became a fearful child and allowed fear to cripple me. All throughout my childhood and into my adult life I would always allow fear to stop me from making decisions or taking risks outside of my comfort zone. I wouldn't step out on faith because I didn't truly understand what faith was about. I now know that there are times when we have to make decisions based on our personal faith and trust in God. I had to learn to take a leap of faith and just step forward, without allowing my fear to paralyze me. My fear used to hinder me from moving in the direction God wanted me to go; I've grown spiritually to realize that fear is not of God, but God has given us love, power, and a sound mind.

When I would come up against something unfamiliar and uncomfortable, I would seek the guidance of people around me whom I felt I could trust. Ultimately, I would accept their opinions of what I should do and act upon their advice, instead of consulting with God. I would confer with other people because I didn't have a real understanding of what it meant to have a relationship with God. I would ask people around me, whether it was family, acquaintances, or someone else from whom I might take advice; however, I didn't think about the source of the advice. I didn't realize that in some cases, I was asking someone about subject matters they didn't have any expertise or experience in. In addition, I didn't know or consider whether the person's motives were pure or in my best interest. Don't get me wrong; it's good to seek the counsel of others when you feel the need to do so, but choose your counselors wisely.

As I have grown closer to God, I now understand that He didn't want me to turn to people when it was time to trust Him. He didn't want me to rely upon myself or the advice and direction of others out of fear and uncertainty. There are many times when God simply wants us to trust Him. Period. I didn't realize I was holding the words of others higher than the words I received from God. I would always justify why I made or didn't make a decision based upon the opinions of someone else. I never took into account the fact that some people didn't always have my best interest at heart. People who didn't want me to succeed could've given me advice to steer me away from my true path for their own selfish reasons. Because of my trusting nature, I would innocently ask for advice from people I respected and trusted, and though many people in my past were well-intentioned when it came to attempting to guide me, I had to learn to put my faith in God and not in man. God allowed my bullying so I would focus on him and not my circumstances, and learn to trust in Him and not people.

I wanted so much to be part of a group, but I was continually rejected. God wanted me to understand and know what it was like to be rejected and what it was like to stand alone and not be popular. As my relationship with God has grown stronger, He's given me more clarity about my whole childhood ordeal. I may have been standing alone physically, but my Heavenly Father was standing with me as my Comforter and my Counselor. I don't regret anything that God allowed me to go through. I wouldn't change anything because that's what has made me who I am today— it was all for Christ's glory.

CHAPTER TWO

An Angry Boy

"THOSE WHO CONTROL THEIR ANGER HAVE GREAT UNDER-STANDING; THOSE WITH A HASTY TEMPER WILL MAKE MISTAKES." (PROVERBS 14:29 NLT)

I was an angry boy who became an angry, prideful, and stubborn male.

When I look back on my early childhood, being bullied and teased caused a great deal of resentment and frustration towards people in general. Due to my lack of understanding, I felt like I'd been let down by everyone around me because I was an innocent child who felt like he didn't have anyone to turn to. Of course, now I know that wasn't true, but I was a hurting child. Very few people came to my defense at the time. I felt alone, worthless, and isolated because I was in the dark about how to express what I was experiencing. I didn't know or understand why I was being treated like an outsider who didn't belong anywhere. My mother and my family didn't have any idea about the turmoil and the torture I felt and endured at school and in the neighborhood. As the bullying and teasing continued, I felt something brewing and festering deep within me.

This unfamiliar feeling wasn't anything I had ever felt before. Being a child, I was afraid of this feeling because of the thoughts that would cross my mind. My anger first began to reveal itself at school and then would flare up away from school as well. In elementary school, I initially responded to the children teasing me by moving to another desk or focusing more intently on my classwork to escape the pain. I was never able to work up the courage to say anything or even stand up for myself.

At home, the one thing my family began to notice was I would become very irritated and short-tempered with my toys; I was beginning to show signs of displaced aggression. I wasn't able to express my anger at the actual source that provoked me, so I took my anger out on the easiest and closest target. I had a great time playing with my Lego blocks by creating figures, but whenever something didn't turn out the way I expected, those same Lego toys would end up thrown against the wall, shattered in pieces. No fault to my family, but they didn't think much of these outbursts, and neither did I.

At about the age of ten, another example of my anger began to surface when riding in the car with my mother. Someone in the car next to us would innocently glance at me as I sat in the passenger seat of our car. Because of my low self-esteem and anxiety, I would give them the middle finger—careful to avoid detection by my mother. That action would usually result in them jumping behind my mother's car and riding her bumper angrily, which in turn caused her to respond in kind. All the while, my mother would have no idea why these people were riding on her bumper and giving her the same hand gesture I had given them. This occurred on numerous occasions until one day she caught me in the act.

On one particular occasion, the car I gave the hand gesture to was occupied by no-nonsense people. My mother parked her car and then exited it to confront the other driver, but I chose to stay in the car because I was afraid. I can't remember exactly what was said, but the occupants of the other car stated that they were upset because I had given them the middle finger. I do remember my mother looking back at me, but I wouldn't look at her. My mother apologized for my actions and fortunately that ended the confrontation, but it also opened the door of discipline for me when we got home.

My acting out and giving strangers the middle finger and many other similar behaviors could've resulted in serious and dangerous situations, but thankfully, they didn't. All of my acting out and behavior problems were because of my displaced anger. God was watching over and protecting me and my family, in spite of me. When I look back on these early incidents of anger, they were the signs of the storm to come. These behavioral incidents were triggered by my low self-esteem and low self-worth caused by the bullying. These behaviors were not the correct way to handle the situations, but I didn't know of any other way to communicate and express my deep pain and inner turmoil.

When I entered junior high school, I was still a shy and non-confrontational child, so the bullying continued. My self-esteem was so low, any time someone would glance in my direction, I'd immediately assume that they were talking about me in a negative way. It was pretty much the same story for me in high school. I took on a few jobs but I was fired from every one because of my temper and lack of respect for authority. As a child, I didn't have a great respect for law enforcement, specifically the Compton Police and the Lynwood Sheriffs.

On one occasion, as a friend and I were walking down the street, a sheriff's car pulled up, and without a reason, they told us to put our hands on their car hood. The car hood was extremely hot, so we pulled our hands away from it. With a few expletives, the sheriffs told us to put our hands back on the hood and not to remove them. They began to search us and remove everything from our pockets and place it on the hood of the car. After they didn't find anything illegal, they used a few more expletives and told us to get our stuff off the hood and leave. They never gave us a reason why we were stopped and searched. In my adolescent mind, I saw this incident as another instance of bullying.

During my teen years, my anger would manifest at times as I drove. My mother purchased a car for me when I was sixteen. As I reflect on my temperament and behavior as I would drive that car, I realize I am truly fortunate to be alive today. On one occasion, someone drove too close to my bumper and I had an immediate and extreme reaction. I slammed on my brakes, exited from my car with a crowbar in my hand. I ran to their vehicle, broke their driver's side window, got back in my car, and drove away—all without thinking twice about my actions.

Due to the bullying and teasing, I began missing days of school without my mother's knowledge. In high school, they would attempt to call my home to report my absences, but my mother never received the messages because I would unplug the phone. In the end, I ended up barely graduating from high school with a 1.33 GPA. I disliked school so much that I didn't even attend my own prom or graduation. To this day, I honestly have no regrets about not participating in any of my senior activities. I was just glad to be done with school.

The major turning point in my life occurred when I joined the United States Air Force. I was supposed to join with a guy whom I hung out with all the time, but he caught a hit-and-run felony and ended up going to jail. Later on I would find out that the same guy is serving a life sentence in prison for murder. It would've appeared to anyone on the outside that joining the Air Force was a positive step in the right direction for me. However, enlisting in the military would be the next step of the escalation of my anger. First, let me say that joining the Air Force was definitely part of God's plan. I only took the Air Force qualifying exam to get out of class—and I passed it. Many people around me were surprised I enlisted in the Air Force because I was perceived as an introverted child, and people believed I would end up staying at home with my mother for as long as I could. God has a sense of humor, though, because the military is the last place anyone should've gone with my short temper and lack of respect for authority.

When I entered basic training, my anger began to surface in various disrespectful ways towards the drill instructors. The drill instructors would give me orders, but I simply didn't want to follow them. The bullying had really taken its toll upon my mind to the point I didn't want anyone telling me what I could and could not do and when I could or could not do it. What a place to decide I didn't want anybody telling me what to do. The drill instructors would bark out their orders in my face, but instead of cowering, my face would reflect what I was thinking about them, with raised eyebrows and twisted lips. The drill instructors would always tell me, "You need to correct your facial gestures when I'm speaking to you." I never uttered a verbal response to the drill instructors, but my facial gestures would always communicate my thoughts, loud and clear. It was truly a miracle that I was allowed to graduate from basic training as a military policeman. God truly had His hand upon me.

At the age of eighteen, when I arrived at my first duty station in Victorville, California, I began to take an interest in weightlifting. Due to the bullying in school, I never had the confidence to play any sports or get involved in any type of physical activity. However, as I began working out, I started to notice the change in my body size, and something began to happen to my self-confidence. I vowed at that point never to be a victim again, but I still had a long way to go with my self-esteem issues. This would become very evident as I began to notice how people responded to the dramatic change in the size of my body.

On one hand, it was a great boost to my self-confidence, but on the other hand, there was a negative side to this change. When I perceived that someone might be attempting to bully me, I would respond with a burst of anger. Even if it was discovered later that it wasn't that person's intention to come off that way, I was still very unforgiving. I believe this behavior was the result of feeling helpless and unable to defend myself as a child. I'm in no way trying to justify my actions as being the correct way to respond; I now realize my anger was connected to my past pain.

Throughout my nine years in the Air Force, I continued to use my muscular build as a defense against anyone I perceived as a threat. Unfortunately, there was a lot of unintended collateral damage as a result. Something unexpected had occurred without me realizing it—I had become the bully. Compounded on top of that, people around me wouldn't tell me what I needed to hear; they only told me what I wanted to hear. This was mainly because the people around me knew I had a temper and they wanted to avoid any type of confrontation with me. Often I would go out of my way to instigate these confrontations. There was one particular incident at an Air Force Base Club where I deliberately bumped into someone in an attempt to start a fight with him. As soon as I noticed the fear in the gentlemen's eyes, I slammed him against the wall in view of everyone. In spite of me being in the wrong, I had never felt such an adrenaline rush, and it gave me an overwhelming sense of satisfaction.

For the most part, people thought I was an easygoing person. However, what most people didn't realize was my mind was always in an attack posture—picture the attack stance of a martial artist. I was always on guard, always poised to strike back, and ever vigilant not to become someone's victim. I understand that was no way to live, but my emotional pain ran deep. After accepting Christ into my heart later in life, I learned that I should've been poised to help, not to hurt; poised to bless, and not curse.

Throughout my time in the Air Force, I continued to have bouts of anger and rage. As a result, I incurred various disciplinary actions from my superiors. These actions should have caused me to straighten up, but for the most part, they just made me angrier. Despite all this, I was able to separate from the Air Force with an honorable discharge. After my separation from the Air Force my goal was to become a police officer in Los Angeles. That dream was very short-lived and heartbreaking at the time. Even though I had an honorable discharge from the Air Force, my disciplinary record hindered me from becoming a police officer. In hindsight, being rejected as a police officer was truly a blessing; God only knows what trouble my anger would have gotten me into with a badge to hide behind.

At this point in my life, there didn't seem to be any end in sight for my anger issues. My anger continued in various forms, especially road rage, as it had when I was a teenager. Whenever someone would speed up on my rear bumper, I would immediately slam on my brakes hoping they would hit me. Yes, I know that was foolish behavior, but I couldn't seem to resist the burning urge inside me to react. At other times in traffic, if someone drove too closely beside me, I would intentionally swerve my vehicle towards them without any regard for the consequences.

There have been many times when my anger has surfaced in my marriage, and there's one incident that always comes to the top of my mind. One day I drove my wife and three children to a fast food restaurant and used the drive thru. When I pulled up for them to take our order, the fast food worker asked, "Can I take your order?" I then proceeded to give our food order. A few seconds afterwards, the fast food worker stated, "I can't hear you, sir." Frustrated, I responded angrily, and my reply was totally out of left field. I dropped the F-bomb and sped away from the drive thru and headed home with my family in the car. Needless to say, it was a quiet ride home with me feeling like the backside of a donkey. I didn't have any regard for my family or that they didn't get anything to eat. Once we arrived at home, my wife told the kids to get in her car, and they went back out and got something to eat at the same restaurant. Prior to leaving our home, my wife asked if I wanted something to eat. I said, "No," even though my stomach was growling and I was hungry.

This was not an isolated incident. On many occasions when I

arrived at home, my wife told me that she and the kids felt like they had to walk on eggshells. Unfortunately for my family, my mood would switch like the wind. Thankfully, during all of my temper tantrums, I was never physically abusive towards my family; however, I've come to realize mental abuse is just as bad, or at times, even worse than physical abuse.

This gives you a small glimpse of how the stronghold of anger had me in its grip. As a result, there was a tremendous amount of direct and collateral damage to my family. On one particular occasion, that collateral damage was displayed by my son in a fit of anger at a family outing. When I witnessed his anger, my heart sank with sorrow, because he responded just like I would have. This meant my anger episodes were now being manifested through my son. He was modeling behavior he had seen in me. Until 2004, I hadn't really thought about the origins of my anger. That was the year I received the life-altering call from my oldest sister stating my father had died. The anger I felt at that moment was like no other. God would later use that pain for His glory.

My mother was never an angry person, but it was apparently a different story for my father. I never met my father in person, but I heard stories about his anger and jealousy issues. Presently, I have a totally different perspective about my father because I now understand everyone has a backstory. This isn't to justify any of my angry outbursts, but there's usually a root cause as to why someone behaves the way they do. My anger continued to be a serious issue until I accepted Christ in 2001. This is not to say I don't still have challenges with my anger, but it no longer controls me. There is one thing that still bothers me to this day, and that's when someone aggressively speeds up on my bumper, because my mind perceives that as a form of bullying. I'm still quick to revert back to my painful past of being bullied and teased. I'm continually seeking God's help with this challenge. Thankfully, I'm further along than I once was. My relationship with God has truly given me a center of peace and acceptance of who I am, and to whom I belong. It continues to be a journey, but I'm not the person I used to be. The manner in which I handle people and situations is dramatically different than I did in the past.

I believe that God allowed my control over my anger to be tested one day in 2011. It was a typical day and my wife and I were on our way home from shopping. As we drove by a burrito restaurant in our neighborhood, we decided to stop and get something to eat. As my wife and I walked into the restaurant, there was a guy looking upwards towards the menu. I really didn't pay any attention to the guy; the only thing on my mind was a wet burrito with sour cream. The guy turned towards us and proceeded to look my wife up and down, as if he was checking out *her* menu.

Before I could say anything, he started calling me every swear word in the book. Being the light-skinned person I am, I began to turn red with anger. He then took a step forward and my wife did something that shocked me. She jumped in between us and gently placed her tiny hand on my chest. All the while, the guy was still calling me every name in the book and questioning my manhood. "You're a punk," and "You have to have your woman step up for you?" Use your imagination for the other words. What made my wife's action so powerful was that she placed herself in harm's way to keep me from taking the devil's bait. With her hand still on my chest she began to gently push me backwards towards the door. As this was occurring, I maintained eye contact with the guy as he followed my wife and me outside. After he saw we were leaving, he simply went back into the restaurant. What you're thinking right now is exactly how I felt that day. What had caused that guy to unleash his anger and rage upon me for no apparent reason? I don't have an answer to that in a natural sense, but I believe it was a spiritual attack from the enemy.

When my wife and I got back in the car, I was shaking with anger and in tears. The tears were for the built-up aggression I wanted to unleash upon the guy in the restaurant. I restrained everything I wanted to do to that guy because I didn't want to disappoint God or my wife. That incident was a great victory for me, because I didn't allow myself to be drawn into a fight. I made a conscious decision not to take the devil's bait. Taking the bait would have removed my family's covering of protection. Getting arrested for a felony would've jeopardized my ability to provide for and protect my family.

The simple gesture of my wife placing her tiny hand on my chest kept me grounded and focused on what I had to lose. In my opinion, it was a spiritual attack allowed by God in order to see where I was with my anger spiritually. I really believe God wanted to see if my actions would be in alignment with my prayers to Him about controlling my anger.

On a funny note, after we left the restaurant, the only thing that kept playing over and over in my head was, "All I wanted was a wet burrito with sour cream."

Bullying really took a toll on my entire life, but there's something positive that came out of it. I'm truly more sensitive to the so-called underdogs in life because I know what it's like to be the underdog. The person I've become today stands up for anyone who can't speak for themselves and for those who don't have the self-confidence to do so. I still struggle with my self-confidence at times. Even to this day, when I hear people laughing, part of me struggles not to revert back to my childhood way of thinking they're talking about me in a negative way. Another area of low self-esteem I'm seeking God for help for is that I have difficulty maintaining eye contact with myself in the mirror. My self-esteem has improved, but I'm striving daily through Christ for constant progress.

I also have to be mindful and vigilant in regards to what may trigger my anger. Thank God I don't have the temperament of a grizzly bear like I did when I met my wife almost twenty years ago. She now calls me her "Teddy Bear," because I've grown in my relationship with

Christ. I'm at peace with knowing I'll be a continual work-in-progress until I'm called home to be with my Father in Heaven. I've been able to use my pain, turmoil, and destructive behavior to help others avoid making the mistakes I made. In spite of my weaknesses and brokenness, I accept that I'm in the ongoing process of being made whole through Jesus Christ.

CHAPTER THREE

Risking All for Attention

"DOING WRONG IS FUN FOR A FOOL, BUT LIVING WISELY BRINGS PLEASURE TO THE SENSIBLE." (PROVERBS 10:23 NLT)

My first arrest was in 1986 for suspicion of auto burglary, just before I was to leave for the Air Force. One night about 11 p.m., I snuck out of the house and met up with a couple of guys from my neighborhood. We decided to drive around and look for a car to steal. We ended up driving through the parking lot of an apartment complex, but we didn't find what we were looking for. Upon leaving the apartment complex and heading towards the freeway, we were pulled over by the police. There were three of us in the car and I was riding in the front passenger seat. The driver was eighteen years old, but the guy in the backseat and I were under eighteen. As is all too familiar today, the police had all of us exit the vehicle and sit on the curb. As the police searched the vehicle, they noticed a bag of tools on the front seat; the bag contained a dent puller which is commonly used to steal cars. Fortunately for us, we hadn't been successful in our search for a car to steal that night; however, the police didn't release us—they arrested us. They took the driver to jail because he was eighteen years old, booking him on suspicion of auto burglary.

They didn't take the other guy or me to jail because we were minors. The police transported us to Orange County Juvenile Hall where we were booked on suspicion of auto burglary. They attempted to get in contact with our parents, but my mother was on a trip to Texas. They wouldn't release me into the custody of my older brother or sister because they weren't my legal guardians. What made the situation worse was my mother wasn't on a pleasure trip to Texas; my mother had traveled to Texas to see her dying mother, my grandmother. Once the police were finally able to speak with my mother, they agreed to release me into the custody of my sister. Even though I was only in juvenile hall for a few days, it felt much longer. The parents of the other minor refused to pick him up for a week or so. His parents told him that he was no longer to associate with me at all. They ended up nailing his bedroom window shut because that was how he snuck out of the house.

Prior to this first arrest, my need for attention far surpassed the risk of being caught. Before this incident, I had stolen numerous cars, but there had never been any police involvement. Keep in mind, at the time of this arrest, I was a few months away from going into the Air Force—I was jeopardizing my future. The only thing I can say is God was watching over this fool, because I didn't take the arrest as a warning.

The ride home from juvenile hall with my sister was pretty calm and uneventful. Once my sister and I arrived at home, I jumped in my car to go get something to eat. I drove up the street to a Louisiana Fried Chicken on the corner. In the parking lot, I noticed a car similar to mine. I exited my car and proceeded over to the other car and opened the hood. Before I could take anything from the car, the Compton police pulled up and shined a light on me. They got out of their car, and once again I was handcuffed and placed into the back of a police car.

While I was in the back seat, I noticed a middle-aged man approaching the police. The man ended up being the owner of the car I was breaking into. To my embarrassment, I recognized the man because I had been over his house on multiple occasions to visit his daughter. I couldn't hear what was being said between the man and the police, but I'll always remember the look on his face when he recognized me. It was a look of betrayal and disappointment—a look I will remember for the rest of my life. I just knew I had blown my chances of going into the Air Force. After the police finished talking with the man, they came back to their car and opened the door. They told me to get out of their car and be thankful that the man didn't want to press charges. They removed the handcuffs, said a few expletives, and told me I was free to go. In tears, I jumped in my car and went straight home, feeling the lowest I had ever felt in my life. Twice in the same week, God had watched over and saved this fool.

Even after these encounters, I still continued to steal and burglarize cars without any regard for the consequences. I managed to remain under the radar until I left for the Air Force a few months later. To give you a better understanding of how I ended up as a car thief, I have to start from the beginning and explain why I was risking everything just for attention. Before I begin, I must tell you I take full responsibility for any and all of my actions (past and present). The following is not meant to excuse my actions at all.

I've already established my father was absent from our house, so as a result, I looked up to my older brother. Being a young boy, I wanted to hang around my older brother, but he never seemed to have time for me. In tenth grade, I noticed my brother began bringing home numerous car radios. I inquired where he was getting the radios and he told me he had stolen them. I asked him if I could go out with him one night to get some car radios, but he said no. Because my older brother didn't want me around him, I began hanging around another older guy in the neighborhood who paid attention to me. This was the same guy who was supposed to enter into the Air Force with me. However, as I mentioned earlier, he caught a felony for a hit-and-run accident, and is presently serving a life sentence for murder. When I began to hang around this older guy, we did all kinds of mischievous things. The most memorable things were throwing eggs at people, lighting firecrackers near people, and using sling-shots with ball bearings as ammunition. Our pastime of choice was driving around and using the slingshot to break the windows of busi-nesses in various neighborhoods.

After months of this behavior, I had the bright idea to start using the slingshot to break car windows and steal car radios on my own. With a few successful break-ins under my belt, I began to sell the car radios at school and around the neighborhood. In a short time, I became the man people would come to for car radios and various other auto parts. Even though it was wrong, I was finally getting the attention I'd always craved. In the eleventh grade, I began taking an auto body repair class. In class someone shared with me that you could use a dent puller to snatch the ignition from any foreign car, then use a screwdriver to start the ignition, and you can steal a car.

I had never attempted to steal a car before, but with the new knowledge I had attained, I went out and was successful with steal-ing cars with the dent puller. I began bringing the cars home after my mother had gone to sleep. I brought the cars home so I could take my time to remove the parts without any distractions. Looking back, I now realize my mother could've been arrested for my actions for having stolen cars on her property, even though she was in her bed asleep while I was stripping the cars.

After observing my criminal activities, my brother began to take notice of me. I finally thought I was going to have a relationship with my brother. Unfortunately, it wasn't the kind of relationship I had desired. However, at this point in my life, I didn't care why he was paying attention to me, I was just happy he was beginning to notice me. Even though we never went out to steal cars together, it was the closest I'd ever felt to my brother. We finally seemed to have some-thing in common we could talk about at the end of the day. I took advantage of the fact my mother worked long hours and would go to bed early because she was tired. I didn't see any end in sight for my career as a car thief. I loved the attention it was bringing me. For the first time in my sixteen years of living, I was no longer being bullied or teased. This fueled my ego and made me very careless.

On one occasion, I stole a convertible Mazda RX7 from one of the beach neighborhoods in the city. After stealing the Mazda, I dropped the convertible top and drove it home like it was my car. When I got home, I parked the car behind the garage before my mother left for work. My sister and brother were aware the car was there, but they didn't tell my mother. When she left for work that morning I boldly drove the car to school. Arriving at school, I enjoyed the attention I received for having a new car. Many of my classmates thought it was my car, but others knew it was stolen. I kept that car behind the garage for about three weeks, without ever thinking about the consequences of getting caught driving it. When I decided to get rid of it, I drove it about a mile away from our house and ran it into a pole outside a laundromat.

On another occasion, I brought a stolen car home and parked it in the driveway. When my sister and brother asked me whom the car belonged to, I checked the glove box. To my surprise, I noticed a bulging wallet. I was actually excited for a moment because I thought the bulge was money. My excitement disappeared immediately when I opened the wallet and discovered the bulge was actually a police badge. You would think I would've gotten rid of that car right away. That wasn't the case at all. I stripped the car for whatever I wanted, and then dumped the car later on that evening. I was definitely out of control, but I loved the fact people were paying attention to me.

When it was time to leave for the Air Force, I was ready to make a change in my life—or so I thought. After I completed my Air Force basic training in 1986, I was stationed in Victorville, California at George Air Force Base. Basic training gave me a level of discipline I had never experienced before. However, I still had a problem with someone telling me what to do and where to go. Yes, I know, of all the places to go, the military probably wasn't the best choice for me. Needless to say, I was still an immature and angry male who didn't know what it meant to be a man. I served as a military policeman as an eighteen-year-old guy who was still seeking attention.

About nine months after joining the Air Force, I finally felt settled in the base dormitory. On one particular night before I was scheduled to go to work, I heard music from a party in the dorm. I went down to investigate and they invited me in. That simple invitation was a sign of acceptance in my mind, which fed my need for attention. I remember everyone at the party was drinking alcohol, but I had never had alcohol before. That changed on this night. Someone offered me a large cup and told me it was a Long Island Iced Tea. Out of ignorance and full of ego, I accepted the drink with confidence. Not only did I accept the drink, I drank it all. Mind you, I was scheduled to be at work in about four hours. I began to feel strange afterwards: I had never experienced an alcoholic buzz before. Come to find out, that Long Island Iced Tea had multiple types of hard liquor in it.

A short time later, I went back to my room to take a nap before I had to report to duty. I woke up only to realize the room was spinning. Instead of calling someone and telling them about my irresponsible behavior, I proceeded to get dressed for duty. It took me longer than usual to get dressed, but I finally reported in. Before every duty shift, we're issued our weapons and given a short briefing before being sent to our posts. This is the time when our sergeant would inspect our uniforms and equipment. I just knew that someone would smell the alcohol on my breath or coming out of my pores. To my relief, no one smelled the alcohol, so I was released to head to my post.

After about two hours on post, someone relieved me for my midnight meal, handing me the keys to a military police truck equipped with sirens and lights. At this point in the night, I felt even more intoxicated than I had earlier. To this day, I don't remember how I made it from my post to where I had my midnight meal without having an accident. Returning to my post, around one a.m., and for no reason I can explain—aside from pure stupidity—I turned on the sirens and lights and began speeding around the base. After quite a few minutes of this, I heard someone on the police radio calling me. It was my duty sergeant (angrily), asking if it was me blaring the sirens and flashing lights. I responded, "Roger that." He immediately instructed me to drive to his location at our base of operations. I replied with a playful and uncaring, "Copy that." After the radio call, I turned the sirens and lights off and proceeded to my sergeant's location.

Once I arrived at my sergeant's location, I exited the police vehicle. My sergeant approached me and told me that he had received numerous calls asking why someone was running the sirens and lights at one o'clock in the morning. When my sergeant got close enough to me, he smelled the alcohol and asked if I had been drinking. I told him, "Yes," and I was arrested on the spot for DUI (driving under the influence). I was relieved of my weapon, placed in handcuffs, and taken inside for processing. This is truly another example of God watching over this fool because I was allowed to remain in the Air Force despite this arrest. My punishment was light in comparison to what others received who were disciplined for the same misconduct. I was reduced in rank and had to pay a fine, but I was cleared to return to duty after six months.

In spite of my military punishment, I continued to drink alcohol while underage. For the rest of my time in the military, I felt the need to drink before going out for fun. I soon found out I had built up a high tolerance for hard alcohol. Being the one to risk all for attention, I drank alcohol as a form of liquid courage. When I came around people who knew I drank a lot, they bragged about me to other people. Even though the attention was negative, I accepted it like a badge of honor. I continued drinking heavily throughout my time in the military. I began to actually think this behavior was a normal part of life. Drinking to excess was an adrenaline rush for me and fed my ego. The more attention I received, the more risk I was willing to take.

CHAPTER FOUR

The Sexualized Upbringing

"FOR EVERYTHING IN THE WORLD—THE LUST OF THE FLESH, THE LUST OF THE EYES, AND THE PRIDE OF LIFE—COMES NOT FROM THE FATHER BUT FROM THE WORLD." (1 JOHN 2:16 NIV)

I saw my first naked woman at the age of five, which triggered an unfamiliar feeling in my underwear. That odd and unfamiliar feeling turned out to be an erection. The naked woman I saw was an image in one of my grandfather's "special" magazines. Everyone in my family knew my grandfather kept a secret black bag in his closet. I was curious about the bag because my grandfather's behavior would change every time he pulled a magazine out of it. Being the observant boy I was, I began to notice my grandfather would disappear in the bathroom for long periods of time. I quickly connected the strange behavior, long stays in the bathroom, and the magazines together. When I did, it made me all the more curious and eager to find out what he kept in that black bag. When the opportunity arose, I secretly opened the bag when no one was home. Upon opening it, I saw numerous magazines with naked women on the covers. That first glance into my grandfather's black bag of pornography was the seed that grew into a forest of sexual addiction. My innocent curiosity sparked a fire of lust that would become an unquenchable and unhealthy thirst.

After my initial discovery of my grandfather's black bag of pornography, my cousins and I would sneak a look every chance we could. As a child, my sexual radar seemed to always be on and I didn't have the maturity to understand why. No one ever sat me down and explained anything about sex. Because I didn't know what was proper sexual conduct, I began to notice things in my immediate and extended family. Despite my ignorance of sexuality as a child, I did know I shouldn't be witnessing family members having sex with each other. I'm not sharing these things to shame anyone; these observations are being shared transparently and vulnerably for healing. On numerous occasions, I witnessed these sexual acts, but I never told my mother or grandmother. From a child's perspective, I didn't want anyone to be upset with me nor blame me for anything.

Not being taught God's truth about sex and self-control led me into a difficult struggle with sexual addiction. My struggle caused me to isolate myself due to the shame and guilt of my addiction. The bullying and teasing I suffered as a child would make isolation an easy and comfortable home to reside in later in life.

I began to accept the sexual activity I witnessed within and outside my family as normal behavior. I didn't have any foundational reference for godly, sexual conduct. It would've been beneficial to have a father in my life to guide me down that road. I recall one occasion, when I was six or seven years old, my cousins and I were left in the care of some of my adult cousins. After my mother departed, the adult cousins made us children remove our underwear. Once our underwear was removed, the adult cousins made the boys and the girls lie on top of each other. After we were on top of each other, the adult cousins physically pushed our buttocks up and down to emulate sexual intercourse. I can't remember whether there was any physical penetration, but the damage from this incident would become evident throughout my life.

My mother was never made aware of this incident because of the shame I felt. I didn't realize until a number of years ago, but I was a

victim of child molestation. This fact came to the surface after joining sexual addiction groups to determine the source of my addiction
and to heal. When I finally read the definition for child molestation
as a fifty-year-old man, it brought me to tears.

§ 549.93 Definition of "child molestation."

"For purposes of this subpart, 'child molestation' includes any
unlawful conduct of a sexual nature with, or sexual exploitation of,
a person under the age of 18 years." (https://www.law.cornell.edu/
cfr/text/28/549.93)

I believe I subconsciously blocked out that memory and possibly
others because it was easier that way. In my mind it might've been
easier, but it wasn't healthier in the long run. In another incident
from my childhood, I remember going with my older brother over a
girl's house. I was about eleven years old and my brother was about
sixteen years old. When we arrived at the girl's house, my brother and
the girl disappeared into a back bedroom. They left me in the living
room to watch TV and play with my toy suction gun. After I got bored
with the TV and my toy gun, I went towards the back bedroom. I
slowly opened the door and noticed my brother was naked and on top
of the girl. By this time in my early life, I knew what they were doing,
but I still didn't have an understanding of proper sexual conduct.
Being a kid, I was curious. I walked up to the bed as they were in the
middle of the sexual act. I felt invisible to them because they continued with what they were doing. In an attempt to get their attention, I
pointed my toy suction gun in their direction. They still didn't notice
me, so I shot my brother in the butt with a toy dart. When even that
failed to get their attention, I picked up my dart from the floor and
simply left the room. Though this incident may seem comical, I'm
in no way making light of my past sexual exposure. I feel sharing
this helps to give you a general idea of how my young mind became
increasingly sexualized.

I remember one morning before I entered junior high school,

waking up and discovering my underwear was wet. I didn't have a history of wetting the bed, so I couldn't explain the strange substance in my underwear. As a young boy, I didn't feel comfortable going to my mother about it either. I didn't have a man present in my life, and even if I did, I probably wouldn't have asked him about it. The only thing I remember is hearing conversations of other kids talking about something called a "wet dream." At the time, I believed a wet dream was a sexual rite of passage to begin having sex. It's truly amazing how backwards the world is about giving out sexual information. I later found out my so-called wet dreams were really nocturnal emissions. A nocturnal emission by definition is an involuntary ejaculation of semen during sleep. In my opinion, God provided a natural and healthy way of releasing semen.

I became sexually active in junior high school. That's also the same time I began masturbating. Masturbation wasn't openly talked about, but it was something that was accepted—especially amongst the guys. We didn't say the "M-word" per se; we downplayed it using phrases like, "beat your meat," "pet the monkey," and others. Throughout my whole time in junior high and high school, I had sex with numerous girls and struggled with masturbation. Many guys don't think there's anything wrong with masturbation, even some Christian men.

When I entered the Air Force in July 1986, my sexual appetite increased to a whole new level. In order to satisfy my ever-increasing sexual lusts, I began to sleep around with as many women as possible. My lust didn't have any moral boundaries, so I had sex with countless numbers of married women. Sadly, some of the married women's husbands were known to me. Additionally, I began to indulge in looking at pornography in magazines and on video. My insatiable sexual lust progressed to me convincing girls to allow me to take nude pictures and videos of them. I'm not proud to admit it, but I shared the pictures and videos with the guys I hung around with. I wasn't concerned about the damage I was causing to the girls' reputations. I selfishly boosted my reputation by tarnishing theirs.

In 1990, while stationed in Germany, I decided to come home to marry my high school sweetheart. I sincerely thought I was in love, but now I believe it was selfish lust. My plan was to get married and bring my new wife back to Germany with me. However, after the wedding and the honeymoon in California, I went back to Germany alone and gave in to my sexual lusts once again. I committed adultery on my new wife and I didn't feel guilt or shame, because by this time I was numb to my feelings.

Being the immature male that I was, I never reconnected with my new wife after returning to Germany. It would be some time later I would learn she had given birth to our son. I'll go into more detail about my son in a later chapter.

During my time in the military, until I separated in 1995, I impregnated two women. Not wanting to take responsibility for a child, I selfishly asked both of them to have an abortion. I never thought about the psychological and possible physical effects that this would have on the women at that time or in the future. The only person I cared about was me and how I didn't want any children. I wanted to have sex with as many women as I could, but I didn't want to take the responsibility of stepping up and being a man. Not to make any excuses, but I had no idea what it meant to be a man, let alone a man of God. Of course, it would've been nice to have a man of God to teach me the proper way to conduct myself sexually, but that wasn't the case. Most of the men around me—if not all of them—treated women as objects and not as queens. I didn't have any godly men in my life to show me how to treat women. I rationalized my behavior as being acceptable, but I was being a hypocrite.

There was even a time when I had plans to open a strip club when I got out of the military. That definitely would have catered to my sexual appetite. I used to ask myself how I could tell everyone how much I loved and respected my mother, and on the flipside, I was openly disrespecting and using women for sex. I'm truly thankful to God for his undeserved forgiveness for my treatment of women prior to meeting my current wife. Even though I've been forgiven, my heart is still sorrowful for the pain and destruction I caused many women. I was truly self-centered and oblivious to the magnitude of the consequences of my careless actions. I'm sharing my experiences because I want to encourage some boy or man by letting him know we all have a story and a past. Don't allow the world to keep you from seeking God for your personal healing.

After I separated from the Air Force in 1995, my sexual lust remained steady with no change in sight. The only thing I added was frequent strip club visits, even when I was supposed to be working. Part of me didn't see anything wrong with my sexual behavior. However, there was a battle raging within me I couldn't explain or even begin to understand. I wanted help with my sexual lust, but I didn't know where to begin to look for help.

Sad to say, I ended up getting two more women pregnant. Once again, I didn't take responsibility and asked them to have abortions, and they agreed. My sexual lust continued to rule my life until 2000 when I got engaged. However, despite my engagement, I continued to watch pornography and masturbate often. I would always make excuses to myself as to why I couldn't exercise self-control.

My fiancée had no idea I struggled with sexual addiction. In hindsight, I didn't even know that term existed. I had stopped sleeping around with other women when I met her. In my mind, I believed I was being faithful to her. I was only fooling myself and didn't even realize it. There is no way to achieve sexual satisfaction through masturbation without looking at something visually stimulating or by fantasizing. Of course looking back, I understand by indulging in these actions, I was being unfaithful, though not in the sense of physically lying with other women. However, I was mentally connecting to images of other women I continued to view and fantasize about.

Before my marriage in January 2001, I burned the pictures and videotapes I had of other women from when I was in the military. I wanted to put my past behind me, so to speak, and not carry it into my marriage. After my marriage, I managed to stay away from pornography and masturbation for a while. In February 2001, I accepted Jesus Christ as my Lord and Savior. After a few months of marriage and being a new Christian, everything seemed okay; however, I began to watch pornography and masturbate again. Only this time, my sexual lust was stronger than ever. I foolishly believed being married to the woman of my dreams would stop me from giving in to watching pornography and acting out, but I was mistaken.

I felt like such a hypocrite, not only as a new Christian and a new husband, but as a deacon in the church as well. Just a matter of months into our marriage, my wife became suspicious of my behavior. My sexual interaction with my wife was nowhere near what it should have been. It would be weeks—and sometimes months—before we would come together as husband and wife to have sex.

My wife finally confronted me almost a year into our marriage. She didn't think I was having an affair with another woman, but she knew something wasn't right with me. I finally decided to come clean with my wife about my struggle with pornography and masturbation. Selfishly, I felt relieved to confess to her, but my wife was crushed and deeply hurt. She felt betrayed and lost her trust and faith in me. At the time, I was thirty-three years old, but I had been struggling with sexual addiction for twenty-eight of those years. Part of me still didn't consider it adultery because I wasn't actually committing a physical act with another woman. However, according to the Bible, just looking lustfully after a woman who is not my wife is adultery, so I was committing adultery again. As I mentioned before, there's no way to achieve sexual satisfaction through masturbation without fantasizing about someone.

After my disclosure to my wife, I knew it was time to get some help, but I didn't know where to begin. I started with my church, but there were no programs in place for what I needed. Later I would realize that sexual addiction is the elephant in the room nobody wants to talk about. I began a search on my own and found a few groups like Sex Addicts Anonymous and Sexaholics Anonymous. These groups are based on "The 12 Steps to Recovery," similar to what is used in Alcoholics Anonymous. I attended numerous meetings, but it was a difficult process. I discovered it was hard for me to open up to a group of men. The one thing that brought me comfort was the fact I was in a room full of men struggling with the same type of sexual issues as I was. I wasn't truly optimistic about these groups being able to help me; however, as my relationship began to grow with God, I became increasingly hopeful.

Sharing my struggles openly was definitely something foreign to me. All my life I'd only been around guys who saw nothing wrong with pleasuring themselves without involving a woman. I finally felt like I was on the road to healing and restoration. I began to learn about the tools I needed in order to battle my sexual addiction. The first thing I learned was the addiction cycle: it begins with fantasizing, being triggered, acting out, and then guilt – shame – depression – isolation. I became more conscious of the triggers that would cause me to fantasize and act out. I also learned an acronym that truly helped me, H.A.L.T.S., which stands for *hungry, angry, lonely, tired,* and *sad*. The sole purpose of the acronym is to keep these physical states in mind every day, especially in regards to triggers. I personally found I would be in one or more of these physical states whenever I gave into temptation. I soon realized overcoming this was going to be a difficult journey without God.

When I started going through these 12-step programs, I hadn't truly hit rock bottom with my sexual addiction. The main thing I realized about Sex Addicts Anonymous and Sexaholics Anonymous is they are not Christian-based, and as a result, I still continued to struggle in my marriage due to my indulgence in pornography and masturbation. My wife's trust in me was truly strained and I didn't know how I was going to earn her trust again.

In 2008, my wife and I began attending Cottonwood Church in Los Alamitos California. I continued to attend the 12-step groups off and on, but not consistently. My struggle with pornography and masturbation continued, despite my growing relationship with God. I felt like I was living a double life; I was putting on a false face like I had it all together. All the while I was still so broken inside and I kept trying to fix myself on my own. The major problem I had was keeping my thoughts under control.

Around 2014, I heard about a Christian based 12-step program. I was grateful, because by this time, I was truly ready to begin my recovery. In the meantime, my marriage continued to suffer because I couldn't go for long periods of time without acting out and viewing pornography. My wife and I didn't have any heated discussions about my sexual struggles, but I was missing out on the closeness and connection with my wife God intended for marriage. As I began to attend the Christian based 12-step group, I felt like I had finally found a place that I could call home. I believe that was a result of my growth in Christ and my desire to work towards becoming the husband my wife truly deserved. The name of the group I found is called Celebrate Recovery.

At Celebrate Recovery, I gained important tools to help me with my sexual temptation. Two of the tools that I learned to utilize were: 1) bouncing the eyes, and 2) guarding the eye and ear gates. Bouncing the eyes is simply averting your eyes away from anything that might be associated with a sexual trigger. Guarding the eye and ear gates involves being very vigilant about what you see and hear. I've found these tools to be very effective, but it truly takes time and practice on a daily basis to master them. I'm in no way saying I've conquered my sexual addiction, but I've made some great progress through Christ.

Here are some of the adjustments that I've made in my daily life to avoid triggering my sexual addiction:

1. Avoid television and movies with any type of sex scenes.
2. Unfollow and unfriend anyone on social media who posts anything of a sexual nature or can be interpreted as sexually suggestive, i.e. purposeful cleavage display, etc. I block anyone if necessary.
3. Bounce my eyes away from any woman who makes me want to take a second look. The second look is where the temptation lives.
4. Bounce my eyes away from any outside advertisement with any type of sexual content.
5. Do not engage in any unnecessary social media scrolling.

Implementing these tools was difficult at first; I rebelled and kept watching all types of movies without any regard for my sexual triggers. I began to realize I had to make some major changes in my way of thinking. It was more stubbornness and pride than anything else that kept me from taking the proper steps towards healing. I also had to be mindful while on social media. My failure to be obedient and do what was necessary for healing kept driving a wedge between God and me. Celebrate Recovery helped bring about my willingness to accept help.

The program also helped me recognize my own hypocrisy in my attitude towards those who identify themselves as belonging to the LGBTQ (lesbian, gay, bisexual, transgender, and queer) community. Before I started attending Celebrate Recovery, I was guilty of judging them harshly.

That all changed when I realized that there aren't any degrees of sin; a sin is a sin. God opened my eyes to my hypocrisy of judging others through the open sharing in the men's groups at Celebrate Recovery.

Since I've grown to have more compassion for people, I respond differently when someone says something negative about someone who's gay. Now my response is, "You don't know their story!" I understand now anything could've happened in that person's past to affect their sexual identity. I've learned I'm in no place to judge any one of God's children. Not to say I condone the behavior; I'm simply saying I love all people the same way God loves me, regardless of who they are or what they've done.

The most beneficial thing I've found at Celebrate Recovery is fellowship with other Christian men. Being able to share transparently in a group has been instrumental in my success on my road to recovery.

I prayed to God—many times in tears—asking Him to take this sexual addiction from me, but I still continued to struggle. The periods between me acting out became longer and longer, but I just wanted to be totally free. I was encouraged by 2 Corinthians 12, when God tells Paul that His grace will keep him and that God's power works best in weakness.

As I continued in my recovery, I came to realize my sexual addiction was connected to other behavior and habits I never even considered: overeating, excessive alcohol consumption, being a control freak, my anger, and my codependent behavior. I found going through recovery is similar to peeling back the layers of an onion. This realization was initially disheartening until I thought about it on a deeper level. When most doctors treat illnesses, they usually only address the symptoms, but not the root cause of the illness. I believe the same is true with any addiction. I wasn't making any progress in recovery because I kept addressing the behaviors and not the root causes as well. Once I wholeheartedly sought God for freedom, the root cause and contributing behavioral triggers were slowly revealed to me. It's truly amazing what became obtainable when I began putting my trust and faith in God.

Once I became aware of the things connected to my sexual addiction, I became more transparent with sharing my struggles. The most monumental thing that's occurred after almost twenty years of marriage is my wife told me she's finally beginning to trust me. I'm truly sorry I hurt my wife so deeply, but I didn't know that without God I was such a broken man. My wife was angry with me over the years for continuing to fall into sexual sin. She grew tired of my excuses and just stopped being concerned or even asking at all if I had been sexually sober. I'll never take my marriage purity for granted again, by the grace of God. I'll continue to share my testimony to encourage boys and men who may be struggling with sexual addiction. I'm not totally free from temptation, but my peace lies within God. Temptation will always be present, but it's my choice on how I respond to it.

I totally understand I have to remain vigilant for the rest of my days. God's strength works perfectly in my weakness. I hope it encourages you as well. However, I acknowledge I'm still on the road to recovery. I draw strength and comfort in that my brokenness has been made whole in Jesus Christ. I also draw strength from the Serenity Prayer. It uplifts my soul every time I read it.

The Serenity Prayer

God, grant me the serenity
to accept the things I cannot change,
the courage to change the things I can,
and the wisdom to know the difference.
Living one day at a time,
enjoying one moment at a time;
accepting hardship as a pathway to peace;
taking, as Jesus did,
this sinful world as it is,
not as I would have it;
trusting that You will make all things right
if I surrender to Your will;
so that I may be reasonably happy in this life
and supremely happy with You forever in the next. Amen.

CHAPTER FIVE

Masquerading Manhood

"DO NOT CONFORM TO THE PATTERN OF THIS WORLD, BUT BE TRANSFORMED BY THE RENEWING OF YOUR MIND. THEN YOU WILL BE ABLE TO TEST AND APPROVE WHAT GOD'S WILL IS--HIS GOOD, PLEASING AND PERFECT WILL." (ROMANS 12:2 NIV)

IT WAS ALL A BIG LIE!

I was taught as a boy and into my manhood there were certain things boys and men were never supposed to do. Men weren't supposed to cry, be transparent, be emotional, be humble, or be vulnerable. In addition, it was taboo for a man to say, "I love you" to another man, because people might think you're gay. This was perceived by many men as homosexual in nature. The world told me these traits would make me appear weak. In other words, the world would perceive me as a punk and a pushover if I displayed any of these traits.

I believe this lie inflicted the greatest damage on me because I always felt so conflicted inside, especially as a child. I remember as a child being told, "Suck it up. Boys don't cry." I was called a cry baby on many occasions. Being told this didn't help me during my bullying and teasing days. I would find out later in life these traits were actually strengths and not weaknesses. I would also discover these so-called weaknesses would become the keys that opened my wife's heart to me.

This big lie had a tremendous power over my life until I accepted Jesus Christ as my Lord and Savior on February 25, 2001. On that special day, I cried more than I ever had in all of my thirty-three years of living. As the tears flowed, it felt like a weight had been lifted off me. Up to that point in my life, I had always done my best to fight back any tears and not cry. I didn't want to be perceived as being weak.

Because I believed this lie for so many years, I proceeded to participate in one of the biggest masquerades of my life during my last few years in the Air Force. Let me set the stage for you. I grew up in Compton, California, which is known for its gang activity, though I was never affiliated with a gang (this will prove important later). I was stationed in Minot Air Force Base in North Dakota for the last few years of my military enlistment. Picture me, a muscular twenty-four-year-old man with low self-esteem, an anger problem, and no godly man in my life. When people asked me where I was from, their eyes would light up when I told them I was from Compton. Most people associated Compton with what was shown in the music videos and the negative news coverage. After a while, I began to embrace the perception the media portrayed. I became a wannabe gangster, or as some might call it, a "poser" or a "buster."

While I was in North Dakota, I met a couple of guys from Texas with real gang affiliations. They were both in the Air Force as well and one of them shared an adjoining bathroom with me in the dormitory. I began hanging out with them quite often to play dominoes and drink alcohol. As a result of hanging out with these former gang members, my behavior began to be more reflective of what people believed about people from Compton, that we were all gangsters.

In my off time, I would hang out and drink large amounts of hard liquor and beer. I drank alcohol to put on my mask and hide who I really was. Alcohol became my liquid courage, because I was still a frightened little boy inside. I found I couldn't go out to a club without getting a buzz first. My drinks of choice became Seagram's Gin and Old English malt liquor. I would find out later the father I never knew had left me a gift after all. My mother revealed my father's favorite drink had been Seagram's Gin as well. I had somehow developed a taste for the same brand of alcohol as my father without ever being around him in my formative years.

I also began smoking Swisher Sweet cigars, just to reinforce my masquerade. To further perpetuate my thug life image, I even purchased weapons: an AK 47 assault rifle (fully automatic), an SKS semi-automatic rifle, a Desert Eagle 50 Magnum, and a Lorcin 380 pistol. At one point, I began organizing dance parties with myself as the DJ. The drinking and DJing were ways for me to escape and numb myself because I was out of control. My womanizing and sexual addiction were on full throttle during this time. To add to all of this, my use of profanity was at an all new high.

Once again, God took care of this fool. I involved myself in things that should have resulted in a dishonorable discharge for me. My reckless behavior in North Dakota continued until I separated from the Air Force in 1995. It's truly amazing what I was willing to do and who I was willing to be just to be accepted. Wanting to be accepted was the most important thing to me, whatever the cost, even if it could've resulted in military disciplinary action. The person I appeared to be didn't match the person I was on the inside. The world saw a 250-pound muscular man, but I was just a lonely, confused, and lost boy inside. The boy inside me felt safe and protected by the large muscular frame I had built. I refused to open up to anyone out of fear I would be rejected and looked upon as being weak. I found it difficult to love and care for others because I didn't love myself.

Not making any excuses, but the bullying and teasing in my childhood laid the foundation for my low self-worth, which in turn made me vow to never be a victim again and hide behind a false persona to hide my vulnerability from the world.

CHAPTER SIX

Confronting the Need

"FOR AM I NOW SEEKING THE APPROVAL OF MAN, OR OF GOD? OR AM I TRYING TO PLEASE MAN? IF I WERE STILL TRYING TO PLEASE MAN, I WOULD NOT BE A SERVANT OF CHRIST." (GALATIANS 1:10 ESV)

I wanted everyone to like me at all costs! My need to fit in and be accepted would've psychologically and spiritually killed me had it continued unchecked. I grew tired of living my life to please everyone else, besides myself, but most importantly, God.

The need for acceptance is a basic human instinct—although some people value it more than others. I just wanted to fit in, to belong. In order to achieve that, I often had to present slightly different versions of myself, depending on the environment and in the company I was in. I used to have numerous "versions" of myself—for work or home or even online—all tweaked and modified in order to be accepted in that particular situation. Of course, the question is, was I being accepted for who I truly was, or merely for the version I chose to present of myself? I've jumped through every hoop and worn all the right masks, but it seemed all my efforts were never good enough. I was sick of trying to fit in. I just wanted to feel like I belonged the way I truly was, without a mask.

All my life I've been guilty of allowing the fear of what others might think of me to hold me back from being my most authentic self. However, when I truly and maturely embrace my authenticity, and I calmly speak my truth, though I may care deeply about what others think, their opinions are no longer relevant to me.

When I discovered what brought me joy in Christ, it enabled me to share joy with others. It freed me to no longer give any energy to worrying about the opinions of others. The opinions of others have lost their power over me. They're not a part of me anymore—good or bad. I've separated myself from the influence of others' opinions. I can finally listen to people without feeling anything—anger, pain, fear, or any other emotion. I don't cringe from people's judgement. I don't silence my own thoughts for fear of disappointing anyone. I don't fiercely determine to defy their expectations and prove my worth.

When I was guilty of allowing others to define me, I felt suffocated and powerless. The major lesson I've learned is it's okay to care deeply about what others think; however, I just don't care deeply what they think about me *personally*. What others think of me is no longer a factor in influencing my actions or inactions. I've found as long as I know who I am and to WHOM I belong (Jesus), it doesn't matter how others see me. That's where I've found my freedom!

Where's My Daddy?

"FOR IF YOU FORGIVE OTHER PEOPLE WHEN THEY SIN
AGAINST YOU, YOUR HEAVENLY FATHER WILL ALSO FORGIVE
YOU." (MATTHEW 6:14 NIV)

MY DADDY DIED AND I FELT NOTHING! I felt nothing for him, but I did feel abandoned and angry. He died without me being able to ask one simple question, "Why didn't you want to be part of my life?" My ears just wanted to hear the words, "I love you, Son." With his death, I knew the hope of hearing those words would never be a reality. I was deeply angry and I didn't know how to feel. The void inside me was unreachable. The main thought that came to my mind was my father had stayed with and raised his other children. I believe he kept his distance from me out of spite to get back at my mother. I say that because he was angry at my mother because she had the courage to leave him. He was very physically and mentally abusive to my mother. However, my mother fearlessly and faithfully trusted God and did what was best for her and her children. In my mind, I felt that his ignoring my existence was the only way he felt like he could regain control. I don't think he thought or cared about the impact his actions would have upon my life.

I say this not to bash my father, but he was a womanizer and adulterer who more than likely never had a godly man in his life to guide him along the way. I never blamed my mother for my father's absence in my life. She gave me every opportunity available to her to connect me with my father. Unfortunately, I never had the opportunity to meet my father face-to-face before he died of prostate cancer. Shortly before he died, however, my mother was able to get his phone number from one of our relatives. I called his home and his wife answered the phone and I asked to speak with my father. This was the first and only call I would ever be able to make to my father before he died. Unfortunately, and in a crushing blow to me, he refused to get on the phone. I felt crushed beyond belief because I couldn't understand why my father didn't even want to say, "Hello" to me.

With all due respect to my mother, she did the best she could to provide for her family. I appreciate everything she's ever done. To her credit, I never heard her say a bad thing about my father in spite of his actions. That truly speaks to the character of my mother and her trust and belief in God.

I take full responsibility for all of my actions, but I know my father's absence was one of the major contributing factors of my anger. During my childhood, I'm not sure how often I asked my mother about him. As a child, it didn't bother me when I saw other boys with their fathers; however, that would change as I grew into a man. At times I would wonder what my life would have been like if I had a relationship with my father. Would I have been such an angry man? Would I have been able to avoid an addiction to pornography? Would I have known how to be a father to my son? Only God knows the answers to those questions and many others I've asked.

My non-existent relationship with my father was the main reason why I unknowingly and instinctually continued this cycle with my own son. My son was conceived with my first wife, but I didn't meet him until he was four years old because I neglected my fatherly responsibilities. I married my first wife while I was in the Air Force. I was supposed to take her to Germany with me where I was stationed.

However, although I returned home to California from Germany to get married, I returned to Germany without my new wife. The plan was to set up the new house in Germany and send for her, but that's not what ultimately played out. Without my wife's knowledge, I went back to my old ways of sleeping with every girl I could and I never sent for my wife. In other words, I was openly committing adultery while in the military.

Again, I take full responsibility for my actions, but I found it so easy not to feel anything about the sacredness of marriage. I went on about my life like I wasn't married with a child. Due to my immaturity and lack of follow-through, I didn't give them a second thought. Looking back, I find it alarming I could be so emotionless and selfish. I stayed married in name only and I didn't get a divorce until I separated from the military in 1995.

When I was finally able to meet my son, it was truly a wonderful and memorable moment. From that point forward I began to pick my son up every other week—at least that was my intention. I wasn't as consistent as I could have and should have been. The years progressed and when my son turned eighteen, he disconnected himself from everyone around him, including me. As of the writing of this book, I've only had contact with my son about two times in the last eight years. Because of my relationship with God, my heart has been opened and humbled. I take full responsibility for my role of not being present in my son's life as much as I should have been.

Now, I become emotional when I see a father and a son enjoying each other together. It hurts my heart and brings me to tears because all I want is to be a father to my son. For years I had no idea what that might look like or even how I was going to accomplish being a good father. That was the problem all along; I kept trying to do it with my own power and reasoning. I'm not exactly sure why my son chose to distance himself, but I'll be right here with open arms ready to embrace my son with love and no judgement when he chooses to reconnect. I'm praying I'll have the opportunity to build a relation-ship with my son—something I never had with my father. I'll never give up hope because my faith grows stronger with each passing day. In my opinion, I'm responsible in many ways for his resentment and anger. I'm not sorrowful, but I'm hopeful my son's heart will soften. My trust and faith will remain in God for the day when I'll be reunited with my son.

I had always told myself I would never be like my father, but I ended up continuing the same cycle of abandonment. Around 2008, four years after my father died, my mother wanted to move to Texas for a few years. I told her I would pack up her truck and drive down there with her. After about a day or so in Texas, I kept having thoughts of my father. I was still angry at my father even though he was no longer alive. This prompted me to ask my mother if she knew where my father was buried. My mother told me she didn't know, but she would check with a family member. Once we found out where he was buried, we proceeded to the graveyard. We had a difficult time locating his grave, but when we finally did, I asked my mother if she would give me a minute alone. I felt a strong urging in my heart to pray for my father, but I initially resisted it. I didn't know what I was going to pray, but I began to pray for my father's salvation in Jesus Christ. I prayed my father had accepted Jesus as his savior before he took his last breath. I then proceeded to forgive my father for not being present in my life. Next, I prayed for God to forgive him for the pain and the destruction he caused due to his anger and bitterness. The last thing I prayed at my father's grave was for God to forgive me. I asked for forgiveness for the pain and destruction I had caused because of my own anger and stubbornness. I'm not going to lie and tell you something magical happened after I prayed at my father's grave, but my soul did feel lighter.

Since 2008, I've grown much closer to God, but I still struggle at times with my anger. Thankfully, it's not like it used to be, but I have to remain vigilant and mindful of my temper. Most importantly, however, my faith is in God for continued healing and restoration. I want to take this moment to publicly apologize for subjecting my wife and children to my anger and stubbornness. Since that day at my father's grave, I began to heal from my anger and rage because of my feeling of abandonment. I had always heard forgiveness was powerful, but that was the first time I had experienced it personally.

Not long after I began writing this book, I felt a wave of compassion come over my heart for my father. It made me ask a couple of questions. What was my father's childhood like? Did his father ever tell him he loved him? I would think about these types of questions at times. No matter what the answers are, they by no means give him a free pass for not stepping up to the plate and taking responsibility. However, thinking about my father in this manner helped me open my heart to the fact my father probably never had the guidance of his father as a child. In other words, how could my father teach me to be something he had never been taught to be himself? The love of my heavenly Father has brought me healing and peace with my earthly father—the peace and comfort that I finally know where my daddy is. The cycle of abandonment ends with me!

CHAPTER EIGHT

The Love of My Life

"AN EXCELLENT WIFE WHO CAN FIND? SHE IS FAR MORE PRECIOUS THAN JEWELS. THE HEART OF HER HUSBAND TRUSTS IN HER, AND HE WILL HAVE NO LACK OF GAIN. SHE DOES HIM GOOD, AND NOT HARM, ALL THE DAYS OF HER LIFE." (PROVERBS 31:10-12 ESV)

My wife had to raise four children, but we only had three children—I was her fourth child. I behaved like a stubborn, angry, and selfish child, sprinkled with a large portion of the back end of a donkey. This was the storyline for the first seventeen years of our nineteen-year marriage. Based upon the title of this chapter, I bet that wasn't the opening you were expecting. If my wife hadn't been rooted in Jesus Christ when we got married, she would've divorced me in the first month of our marriage. It was a rocky road in the beginning. Within our first year of marriage, my wife would discover me in the fetal position crying like a child, I would file for bankruptcy, my pornography addiction would be revealed—all of which would leave my wife feeling bamboozled.

Before I go there, let me go back to the beginning of how we met. I met my wife in 1996 through an introduction by her sister, Keisha, who was a co-worker of mine at the time. Keisha and I, along with another guy (Steve) were hanging out at their apartment one evening, drinking alcohol. After a short while, I noticed someone walking from the back room. It was a woman I'd never seen before. She and I made eye contact and she said, "Hello," to which I replied with my own, "Hello." This is a standard exchange when two people meet each other; however, that wasn't my normal, so-called manly reaction. My macho twenty-eight-year-old male greeting to a woman at the time was usually a pick-up line: "What's up girl? Is your husband married?" In this case, my wife's simple, "Hello," pierced my false bravado like a hot knife through butter. Prior to my wife (Debra) entering the room, I was drinking and swearing like a sailor. After she walked through, I actually felt uncomfortable, which was immediately evident to Keisha and Steve. At the time, I couldn't explain the emotional impact her simple greeting had on me. Years later, God would reveal to me I was shaken to my core when I first saw my wife Debra because she was the woman He had created just for me.

Another major thing making it a memorable moment for me is she didn't judge me based on my appearance. She saw straight through my false bravado and saw the lonely little boy hiding inside. Her five-second greeting will always be a special milestone in my life. It was the day I was introduced to my true love. I had become accustomed to responding to women out of lust, and had no idea what true love felt like until I locked eyes with my future wife in 1996.

My wife had a different reaction to our meeting. She just kept going about her day and didn't give me a second thought. That heart-shifting moment was definitely not reciprocated by her. However, I believe God wanted to make her simple "Hello" memorable and significant for me. It was so significant, after meeting my wife, my instinct was to run because I didn't feel comfortable keeping up the false front in her presence.

As time passed, Keisha continued to be one of my hanging buddies. At some point in 1997, I finally got my wife's phone number. Debra was travelling back and forth between northern and southern California at the time. I began to call her from time to time to check on her. Even though I was just checking on her, part of me was secretly hoping those conversations would grow into something more. I continued to call my wife until I worked up the courage to ask her out on a date on October 11, 1999. I went all out and our first date included a limo ride to a popular club in Los Angeles. We had an amazing time that evening, so we had a second date on October 23, 1999. This was a lunch date at an Italian restaurant in Santa Ana, CA. Our second date was an overwhelming success as well. Little did my wife know, but I had already begun planning my wedding proposal after our first date.

I had every step planned out. I began by going to a popular jewelry store and choosing a ring. Next, I met with her father and asked for his permission to marry his daughter on February 12, 2000. After careful planning, I was ready to propose on May 7, 2000. The proposal began with a romantic helicopter ride to Catalina Island, a small island off the coast of southern California. My plans included having some of our closest acquaintances travel to Catalina prior to our arrival. Upon our arrival, they held up a banner with the question, "Debra, be mine for eternity?" My wife was overcome with happiness and she said, "Yes!" After that amazing day on Catalina Island, we were married January 20, 2001 at a winery mansion in Ontario, CA. As you can see, I didn't waste much time between our first date in October 1999 to our wedding in January 2001. It never crossed my mind my wife might say no to my marriage proposal. I had a deep feeling within my heart and soul she would say yes. I knew I wanted her to be my wife and I wanted to be her husband.

Every coin has two sides, as does my marriage. I shared the beautiful and romantic story of how my wife and I met and the elaborate proposal to show I truly had all intentions of being the husband and man my wife deserved. However, there was another side to our relationship, and shortly after our wedding, my wife would soon encounter the first warning signs of my spiritual immaturity.

After we returned home from our engagement day excitement, my wife and I enjoyed a conversation together. The atmosphere was cheerful and upbeat and my wife asked something profound, "Would you be upset if I told you I love Jesus more than I love you?" My reply outwardly was, "No, that wouldn't bother me." However, my wife knew by my tone and facial expression my words and face didn't agree with each other. At that time, I couldn't believe I was angry and jealous of her love for Jesus. As I matured in my relationship with Christ, I would later understand it was my selfish need and desire to be the center of attention that caused my anger. Later on in our marriage after my relationship with Christ had deepened, I asked my wife a question, "Would you be upset if I loved Jesus more than I loved you?" She said, "Of course not." Reflecting on the first time that question was posed in our marriage, we had a good laugh together, grateful for how far we had come.

Getting to that point was a difficult journey. Within a month of our wedding, my wife came home to a dark house. She slowly opened the front door and all she could hear was sobs from the darkness. She turned on the lights and discovered the sobs were from her new husband crying in his recliner chair. I was crying because I was days away from filing bankruptcy—a fact I hadn't disclosed to my wife before we were married.

After filing bankruptcy, my wife told me she felt like she had been bamboozled because I had projected an image of financial stability and security to her. I don't make any excuses for my deception, but it wasn't my intention to hurt my family. All of my life, up until I met my wife, I had been a *male* masquerading as a *man*. Even deeper than that, I was still a lonely, bullied little boy inside. A boy who just wanted to be loved and accepted. Had I been honest about my financial situation, there was a chance she might have chosen not to date me, and she certainly wouldn't have married me. Simply stated, I was still that little boy who was plagued by the abandonment of his father, afraid of being abandoned again.

The next major challenge in our marriage arose when my wife began to notice we weren't coming together as often as we should as husband and wife. After my wife confronted me, asking me why I had been sexually distant, I reluctantly told her I had a problem with pornography. That disclosure devastated my wife. She began to question whether there was something lacking in her or if she was inadequate in some way. No matter how I tried to convince her my pornography addiction was not her fault, but was due to my inability to exercise self-control, she still was crushed.

After we got married, I selfishly and blindly believed I could stop my pornography addiction on my own. That was the most misguided thing I could've believed. Addiction is a lack of self-control, so how could I exercise self-control to stop? Part of my problem was I believed pornography wasn't adultery since I wasn't being sexually active with another woman. It took seeking professional help to open my eyes, and to my surprise, Jesus laid it out plain and simple in the Bible, and told his disciples if they even looked at a woman with lust in their eyes, they had already committed adultery. With that knowledge, I had to come to terms with the fact I had committed adultery on my wife countless times.

I began to seek assistance from various worldly and Christian groups so I could be delivered from my sexual addiction. It's been a long and exhausting battle, but by the grace of God, I finally have victory over it. Because of the duration of the struggle, my wife lost trust in me; I was continually falling into temptation due to the stronghold my sexual sin had on me. I would always make excuses to her—and myself—that I couldn't control myself. Through prayer, exercising self-control, and patience, I began to experience victory over my sexual addictions.

I'm happy and overjoyed to report in late 2019, my wife told me she was beginning to trust me again. Up until that point, she resented me and was angry with me because of my failure to take responsibility for my sexual sin. However, in 2019, my wife told me, "You're very transparent and vulnerable now." In the past, the world told me these very traits were weaknesses. As my relationship grew stronger with God, I quickly realized the world had lied to me. The forgiveness by my wife was a direct result of me being transparent and vulnerable with her. My wife felt the genuineness of my total surrender to Jesus Christ, through my consistent actions. She saw I was truly trusting God with my life. That moment brought me to tears because I finally felt like I was being the godly husband she deserved.

Throughout most of our marriage, I felt I was not living up to my potential as a leader in my home. Because of my failure to take my rightful place, my wife had to step up and be the covering over our household—which was out of line with the Word of God.

Due to my immaturity and spiritual struggles, my family was subjected to my daily mood shifts. My wife even told me they felt like they had to walk on egg shells around me. My family even came up with a nickname for me, "Grizzly Bear." The situation got so bad our pastor and his wife had to come to our home to counsel us. The counseling was more like an intervention for me because of my denial of any wrongdoing and refusal to make any changes in my behavior.

It was never my intention to cause pain and anguish to my family. I was a little boy trapped inside a male's body, responding to my family and the world out of my brokenness. I didn't have any idea what it meant to be whole. That would change once I totally surrendered every area of my life to Jesus Christ. I had to come to terms with the fact I had many character flaws that could only be corrected by turning to Christ. It saddens me to say it, but I believe God knew my wife was the only woman who would be able to motivate me to change my life.

She was like my John the Baptist; in a sense, she cleared the way for me to be delivered. God knew I needed my wife and no one else.

No other woman could have brought out the things hidden deep within me. He knew my wife held the key to helping me become the Kingdom man I was created to be. My wife has helped me become more effective in every area of my life. Without my wife, I wouldn't be the man I am today. According to the Bible, my wife was created to be my helper as I follow Christ. I've found she's helped me meet the expectations of what God has for me, to fulfill the purpose placed within me, and serve my generation. In spite of me, my wife loved me, and she demonstrated true godly love as described in 1 Corinthians 13.

I always hear behind every good man there's a good woman. I'm not in agreement with that statement. If my wife was behind me, that wouldn't line up with the Bible. In my opinion, if woman was created from the rib of man, why should she be behind him? If she is behind him, you could make the assumption she was created from the backbone of man. Even though there is truth to women being the backbone of men as a source of support and strength, God's intention was to position woman on the side of man. This embodies man protecting, guiding, and covering his wife as she's standing next to him. It's truly amazing how the world can twist the truth of God's Word when it comes to the purpose for men and women.

I had to share a few examples of how powerful my wife is and has been through Christ. I say, "a few examples," because the list of examples to draw from is extensive. I wanted to give you an understanding of the extent of the pain I put my wife and family through. Without God, our marriage would not have survived. I would have given up and taken the perceived easy road of the world and left, ending up an even angrier, more selfish, and more stubborn single male. I would have been a male destined to be alone and more deeply rooted in the sin of sexual immorality, and God only knows what else.

My wife and I have had some amazing years together, but I had to share some of our most significant challenges. Because of where I am with my relationship with God, I take full responsibility for all of the pain I caused my family. I'm so thankful I serve a merciful and forgiving God. Our marriage today is truly an example that God can make a way out of no way.

One thing that has tremendously helped me to treat my wife as God intended is since 2009, I've carried a picture of my wife as a baby in my wallet. You may wonder why this has helped me and why I do this. One of the Christian men's courses I completed taught me if I can see my wife how God sees my wife—as a delicate, precious, and vulnerable gift from Him—I will treat her as such. The baby picture is meant to symbolize the innocence I've been entrusted with. That picture is a powerful and beautiful reminder of her true worth.

I can say with confidence I've finally taken my rightful place in my household, according to the Kingdom of God. I'm no longer behaving like a lonely little boy; I'm finally standing as the Kingdom man God created me to be.

I've learned to quickly forgive and overlook offenses. I've learned to act in a manner worthy of receiving honor. I've learned to treat my wife with consideration and respect. I've learned to be careful and not to be harsh with her. I've learned to be a provider for my family. I acknowledge and accept I've been anointed to be the spiritual leader of my family.

Just recently, I was finally able tell my wife she's my best friend. I shared with her I hadn't called her that before because I knew I wasn't treating her like a best friend should. I didn't realize how bound I was until I finally allowed myself to be transparent and vulnerable with her. Without my wife, I wouldn't be the man I am today, through Christ. I'm truly thankful for my wife continuing to love me in spite of me. Words can't express how appreciative I am my wife trusted God and exercised unbelievable patience with me. Regardless of what we've endured, our love appears to be growing stronger and stronger with each passing moment.

CHAPTER NINE

Finding a Home

"SEEK THE KINGDOM OF GOD ABOVE ALL ELSE, AND LIVE RIGHTEOUSLY, AND HE WILL GIVE YOU EVERYTHING YOU NEED." (MATTHEW 6:33 NLT)

I'd be DEAD or in PRISON if it wasn't for the prayers of my grandmother, my mother, and my wife, and by the grace of God. Even though I grew up in the church, I didn't embrace the rituals of most churches. I was baptized during my childhood but I didn't have an understanding of what that meant. Quite simply, watching hypocritical Christians is what kept me from seeking and building a relationship with God.

I didn't realize I had allowed the Enemy to redirect my focus on the actions and inactions of people, rather than on God. Please don't get me wrong, I'm not coming from a stance of self-righteous judgement on others. I now acknowledge I'm a sinner saved by God's grace and mercy.

I've never been a big fan of anyone who practices the "do as I say, not as I do" lifestyle, inside or outside of the church. In my mind, that seemed like what the church was all about, and I didn't want to have any part of it. In other words, I was distracted and discouraged by faking and shaking Christians. They weren't fooling God; they were only fooling themselves. That's another sad, but true reality still applicable and evident in churches today.

My distrust of the church was due to the actions and behavior of many of the pastors I had encountered. The majority of the pastors I came across were mainly focused on money and not God's people. They were quick to preach a "name it and claim it" message focused on prosperity, but slow to minister hope, salvation, and love to people.

During this time in my journey, my study of the Bible wasn't consistent. I would read from time to time, but I didn't have a daily regimen of focused reading, study, and meditation on the Word of God. Although I did not have a relationship with God, I still had a deep sense of what was right and true. It was a feeling and understanding I've always had, as long as I can remember, but could never explain where it came from.

Whenever I did take the time to visit a church, most times it was a disheartening experience. My disappointments and frustrations were usually a result of the unnecessary rituals during the service that led to long, drawn-out church services. My disenchantment with the church and fake Christians continued until I was delivered from my blindness on February 25, 2001 and my heart, mind, and spirit were opened to the truth.

Up until that point, my focus had remained on hypocritical Christians and the religious rituals of the church. Come to find out, I had fallen for the biggest lie and distraction of the Enemy—a lie which kept me from the truth of my salvation. The truth came when I finally realized salvation had nothing to do with the actions or inactions of others who claimed they belong to God. In actuality, salvation had *everything* to do with *my* personal relationship with God. This truth only came to me when I began to actively study God's Word for myself.

I chose to no longer focus on how I believed other Christians should behave and judge their relationship with God. It reminds me of the story of Martha and Mary in the Bible. Martha was so concerned about what she believed Mary should be doing. Her misplaced concerns about Mary hindered her from doing her own duties. In my case, I was Martha, because I was too concerned about how I believed others should worship God.

My spiritual journey took some time and years for me to reach my day of salvation on February 25, 2001. My wife, however, already had a strong relationship with God. She had been attending two different churches for many years, though she hadn't joined either one. She attended Greater Mount Sinai Missionary Baptist Church #2, in Compton California, which was pastored by Pastor Kalvin and Lady Pamela Cressel. My wife also attended Cottonwood Church in Los Alamitos California under the leadership of Pastor Bayless and First Lady Janet Conley. After we were married, my wife continued the same pattern of visiting both churches from time to time, but I didn't attend with her. She never pressured me to attend any church services with her. Looking back, I know she was praying for my spiritual growth every day. My wife's genuine love for Christ and consistency of church attendance made me curious about God.

My curiosity didn't immediately lead me into the arms of Jesus. I was still a prideful, stubborn, and selfish man-child who didn't want to change. Coming to the end of myself is what made me more receptive of my wife's godly example. Although I was setting high goals and achieving them in my personal and professional life, I still felt empty inside. I was empty because I needed God in my life, but He was slowly drawing me closer and closer to Him.

I pursued what the world always told me would make me successful. That included owning numerous rental properties, owning a real estate brokerage, and lots of cash in the bank. However, even though I had the things that were supposed to make me happy, there was still a black hole within me. I would later realize that emptiness could only be filled by God.

As my wife continued to attend church, I decided to tag along with her on one particular Sunday to visit Greater Mount Sinai Missionary Baptist Church #2. We arrived at the church and we were greeted with love. I truly felt welcomed, but there was a battle going on within me I couldn't explain. I felt uneasy and anxious and wanted above all else for the church service to be over. My feelings had nothing to do with the pastor or the congregation. It had everything to do with the struggle I was fighting within my soul.

As we approached the end of the service, Pastor Cressel asked if there was anyone there who would like to accept Jesus Christ as their Lord and Savior. I began to sweat profusely, which prompted my wife ask me if I was okay. I told her I was fine, but she knew otherwise. I had a strong urging within my soul to accept Jesus Christ into my heart, but I refused to go to the altar on that particular Sunday.

A couple of weeks or so went by and I decided to attend Greater Mount Sinai with my wife again. Just as before, we were greeted with love and I truly felt welcomed. Once again, as the end of the church service neared, I began to sweat profusely. At that point Pastor Cressel asked if there was anyone who would like to accept Jesus Christ as their Lord and Savior. My wife and I were both facing the front of the church where Pastor Cressel was standing. I was standing on the right side of my wife and the walking aisle was to the left of my wife. Pastor Cressel then repeated, "Is there anyone who would like to accept Jesus Christ as their Lord and Savior?" My wife turned her head to the left towards the walking aisle. She then turned her head to the right to look at me—only to find out I was no longer standing there. This particular day I could no longer ignore the strong tugging on my heart from Jesus Christ. With each step I took towards Pastor Cressel, I began to feel the weight of the world being lifted off of me—a weight and a burden I shouldn't have been carrying in the first place.

By the time I finally made it to the altar and stood before Pastor Cressel, I was already crying uncontrollably and shamelessly. I didn't have any regard for who saw me crying or what they thought of me. This was a significant moment for me because I was always concerned about what people thought of me. However, on that day, there was a peace that washed over me, a peace I had never felt in my life. I now understand I was experiencing God's love and peace welcoming me into His Kingdom.

Prior to that Sunday when I gave my life to Jesus Christ, I was spiritually bankrupt and at the end of myself. I tried to fill my emptiness with worldly wealth and things I accumulated; however, material things couldn't fill the God-shaped hole in my soul. At one point I even loved money more than the company of people. Most of the people in my life during that time were only around me because of my money anyway. This is why I felt alone, even when I was in a room filled with people.

I would even go as far as to say money and the pursuit of it were gods and idols in my life. I'm in no way saying there is anything wrong with having money. It all depends on your motives in obtaining it and the methods by which you obtain it. In my case, my motives were based upon selfish gain and selfish ambitions. Many people will often misquote the Bible and say money is evil. Money isn't evil in and of itself. The Bible actually states that the love of money is the root of evil. There's nothing wrong with having the money, it's whether or not the money has you. My money most definitely had me bound, lost, and lonely.

That was a life-changing year for me—a change for the better. In 2001, I got married to the love of my life in January. In February I accepted Jesus Christ as my Lord and Savior. March 2001 I decided to file personal and business bankruptcy. This mirrored the spiritual bankruptcy I was experiencing at the same time. Prior to accepting Christ, I had lived thirty-three years with spiritual blinders on. When I accepted Christ, the blinders disappeared and they no longer hindered my spiritual vision. I gained mental clarity, which led me to make the decision to file for bankruptcy. This action was a way for me to show God I wanted to start over again with Him as my solid rock foundation. I vowed not to be like the rich young ruler who is mentioned in the Bible. He will be remembered as the one who loved his possessions more than he wanted to trust God with his life.

Prior to accepting Jesus Christ as my Lord and Savior, I had built everything on an unstable foundation of sand. I was used to living my way, on my own terms, and without apologies. As a result, the life I had built on that faulty foundation fell and came crashing down around me.

After I surrendered my life to Christ, I joined Greater Mount Sinai Missionary Baptist Church, and that action caused a divine chain of events for my family in the ensuing months of 2001. My wife made a decision concerning a church home and finally decided to join Greater Mount Sinai MBC as well. Not only her, but my son and my mother also joined, and they all were baptized that same year.

We were members Greater Mt. Sinai MBC for a number of years. As we continued to grow in the Lord, our spiritual journey has progressed and my wife and I are now members of Cottonwood Church in Los Alamitos, CA. My journey of faith and trust in God will continue until I'm called home to be with my Father in Heaven. It's been a very challenging yet rewarding journey. I wouldn't change anything about my past experiences. They all contributed to where I am today.

My peace of mind didn't begin until I came to the end of myself. When I began to trust God, I finally found a home in the arms of Jesus, and not the world. I no longer feel alone; I'm truly at peace within my soul.

CHAPTER TEN

Hope

"'FOR I KNOW THE PLANS I HAVE FOR YOU,' DECLARES THE LORD, 'PLANS FOR WELFARE AND NOT FOR EVIL, TO GIVE YOU A FUTURE AND A HOPE.'" (JEREMIAH 29:11 ESV)

From 2001 to 2016, I binged on a rollercoaster Christian life of disobedience and fear. My disobedience hindered me from living and growing in line with the Word of God.

I allowed fear to paralyze me from stepping forward in faith, which in turn made me afraid to step out of my comfort zone and obediently trust God. I was guilty of believing the popular expressions that said, "You have to have a Plan A and a Plan B," and, "You have to think outside of the box." I had to come to the realization my God didn't operate within the boundaries of my self-imagined and self-constructed plans.

My belief is God never intended for me to have a Plan A and a Plan B; He only intended for there to be a Plan A, which is have faith in Him. Having a Plan B always allowed me to retain some sense of control, just in case the Plan A didn't work out the way I wanted it to. In order to progress in my Christian walk, I knew I had to stop believing the lies of the Enemy. I had to start walking in faith and trusting God if I was ever going to be truly free.

I had to learn to trust God with everything within my soul, regardless of the fear and uncertainty I felt. I was striving to exhibit courage, but my understanding of courage was wrong. I had always believed being courageous meant you were not afraid. I soon found out courage isn't the absence of fear; it's choosing to move forward in faith and trust God *in the presence of fear*. How powerful is that?

Nothing changed in my life until 2016 when I humbled myself and totally surrendered my will to God! In other words, I had to stop being a control freak and trust God to take full control of my life. I had to get off the high horse of my ego, pride, denial, immaturity and stubbornness. Most importantly, I had to stop living and hiding behind my past successes and begin living in the present for God. I was getting lost in my own praise. I had to stop smoking my own exhaust, which was fueled by my own selfish achievements.

After coming to the end of myself in 2016, I began to sincerely seek God's purpose for my life. An integral part of God's purpose for me was to develop healthy relationships with other godly men to help me in my faith walk. Because of years of self-imposed isolation and social awkwardness, this was a difficult task; however, no matter how I felt, I knew I needed the fellowship of other Christian men. My wife mentioned there was a Christian men's gathering at Cottonwood Church on August 20, 2016. At first I was reluctant to buy a ticket because of my desire to retreat to my old patterns of isolation and sexual addiction. I overruled my fear and stepped forward in faith; I finally made the choice to stop playing the victim and walk in the victory of Christ.

I successfully made it to the men's gathering, hopeful for what I might learn, but I was turned off by one of the pastors present. This particular pastor began to share a racially charged story that was totally out of line for a church setting. As the pastor shared the story, I noticed how uncomfortable it made many of the men from different ethnic backgrounds. The pastor seemed not to care about the inappropriateness of his message, but I was very concerned about how the story could affect some of the men there. That pastor's irresponsible behavior could've changed someone's mind about accepting Christ that day.

Turned off by the pastor's remarks, I was fully distracted and turned my attention to my smartphone. (Yes, I know I should've kept my focus on God and not on man.) As I began to scroll through Facebook, I noticed the app offered a video slideshow option. This feature allowed anyone to create a personal video with their photos and add background music. As I began to create a slideshow, I felt something difficult to explain: I began to feel excitement and peace at the same time.

Little did I know at the time, but this distraction led to a remarkable discovery. Creating my Facebook slideshow story on a presumed whim sparked the fire of creativity and curiosity that had been sleeping inside me all along.

As I sought out more knowledge about video creation and editing, I began to soak up everything I could find on the Internet. I took the knowledge I was learning and began to hone my skills. In addition, I began fellowshipping with other Christians outside of church. On one particular day, after the Cottonwood Church Men's Gathering in March 2017, I noticed an advertisement for an upcoming book release for Stephanie Shelling's book, *Afraid to Live: Confessions of a Believer Who Didn't Trust God*. I had never met Stephanie in person; we were only friends on Facebook, so I was somewhat reluctant to show up at her book release. However, as soon as I entered the church, I heard a voice in the distance say, "Hey, everybody, that's my Facebook friend." I immediately felt more at ease. God used Stephanie on that day. Her simple greeting made me feel so welcomed. We never know the lasting impact we have on people with the simplest of gestures.

My goal at the time was to get out of my shell of isolation by doing the opposite of what I felt inside. In other words, I forced myself to do things I've always been uncomfortable doing. In this case it was meeting and fellowshipping with people I didn't know, which was well outside of my zone of comfort and control. However, this ended up being a God-ordained meeting; He was guiding my steps that day. I had no clue May 6, 2017 would mark the birth date of my mental and spiritual creativity. Quite simply, that day was a day of revelation—I finally discovered what I was created to do. It was revealed I had the gift of creativity. This revelation provided the foundation of my video production, video editing, and aerial drone business. Just think, I had been searching for my gift outside of myself and it had been with me since birth.

My life changed at Stephanie Shelling's book signing, in part due to meeting a gentleman by the name of Laval Belle, the publisher of Stephanie's book. I purchased a copy of her book and also available for purchase were books Mr. Belle had written. After purchasing and reading his book, *Your Gifts Are Not Your Purpose*, one of the Bible verses he references, Proverbs 18:16, remained at the forefront of my mind. It states, "Your gift will make room for you and bring you before important people." I took this verse to heart. I began to humble myself and started exercising my gift, and doors of opportunity have begun to open for me, all because I am exercising my God-given gift of creativity. Through it all, God has and will continue to receive the glory, not me! An important lesson I learned from this experience is it's never too late to pursue your gift.

If you're having difficulty figuring out what your gift might be, keep it plain and simple! Please don't be like me. I made it difficult for over fifty years of my life, chasing after money, jobs, and position. Ask yourself what's the one thing you enjoy doing above anything else, and if you could make a living from it you would. Think of the thing you love to do for the pure joy of doing it and it doesn't feel like work. It may be simple to pinpoint that thing, but it's not always easy to pursue our gifts and talents. Believe me, I understand; I had to ask myself what price I was willing to pay for my peace of mind.

I believe you're awesome and powerful! You can do whatever you put your mind to do! We all have a God-given gift, but I had to humble myself and step out of my comfort zone and stop being paralyzed by my fears to recognize my gift. Everyone else around me recognized my gift, except me! But it's never too late! I share this with all transparency because I want you to live your life with fulfillment by exercising your God-given gift. You can do it! We weren't created just to exist, but to glorify God. Our gifts are supposed to be used to serve people for God's glory. Don't let your fears paralyze you; allow them to propel you in the direction calling you from deep within.

After attending Stephanie's book release, I officially established Purpose Video Services—a video production, video editing, and aerial drone company. At that point in my life, I had been a licensed real estate broker for almost twenty years. I had achieved some substantial success early in my real estate career, but it was short-lived. I began my real estate career in 1997 with Century 21 Results in Lakewood, CA. I was named Rookie of the Year and was awarded numerous awards for being a top salesman. In addition, I began to invest in real estate and I built up a nice portfolio of rental properties in Long Beach, CA. From the outside, it appeared like I was the epitome of success, but I was lost, lonely, and empty inside. My sense of peace and joy didn't come until I accepted Jesus into my life. That was the same year I filed personal and business bankruptcy. I continued to work in the real estate business full time after my bankruptcy, but I always felt like I wasn't living up to my potential. It was usually a feeling of, "There's got to be more to my life." I was confused about my purpose because my relationship with God wasn't what it should've been.

When the real estate market crashed in 2008, I had to get back in the job market. I ultimately ended up working at the U.S. Military Processing Station in El Segundo, CA. I remained on that job for nine years, but I continued to sell real estate to my existing and past clients.

It came to a point where I had to make a decision about leaving that job because it was not fulfilling to me. My peace of mind was at an all-time low; I was depressed and I didn't know it. I finally came to the realization I couldn't serve two masters. I wanted to pursue my God-given purpose of creativity, but I had no idea what that would look like financially.

I made the decision to trust and serve God, so a took a leap of faith. I submitted my two-week notice and resigned from that job on December 21, 2017. I stepped out on faith with no monthly income, aside from my monthly $260 veteran's disability payment. Financially it was extremely tough for my family at first, but God has supplied all of my household's needs. Even though the Bible tells us not to worry, I believe I was the Worry King.

Through it all, since quitting my job and starting my own business, I've experienced the most growth since I began my walk of faith. Of course, it's an ongoing process, but my peace of mind, joy, and living in my purpose are priceless. The only regret I have is I wish I would've taken the leap of faith much sooner. However, I've come to understand God's timing is perfect. As I reflect on the last few years, I can see God was guiding me step-by-step to where I am now. Looking back, I can see with each significant event, I was coming more intentional with my trust and faith in God. You can see that in the timeline of me discovering and walking into my gift:

▸ **August 20, 2016:** I attended the men's gathering at Cottonwood Church—the event that sparked my creativity.

▸ **May 6, 2017:** I attended a book release and met Stephanie Shelling and Laval Belle. This is where my gift of creativity was placed into motion, based upon Proverbs 18:16 (ESV): "A man's gift makes room for him and brings him before the great."

▸ **June 1, 2017:** I officially established Purpose Video Services, a creative video production company for business owners and entrepreneurs, providing TV/Video/Film editing and aerial drone video and photography services. The inspiration for and the foundation of my business is my creative gift (www.PurposeVideoServices.com).

▶ **September 9, 2017:** Because of my creativity, I was asked to join the staff of Laval Belle's publishing company, Noah's Ark Publishing, as their videographer and video editor.

▶ **December 21, 2017:** I resigned from my job and stepped out on faith to pursue my gift of creativity.

▶ **March 25, 2020:** I began writing this book three years after being introduced to Laval Belle.

▶ **April 17, 2020:** I'm currently developing an online course called Drone, Film, Edit 101, for anyone who wants to learn the basics of flying drones, filming, and video editing (DroneFilmEdit101.com).

I truly believe that I had to match my faith with action to make any lasting and sustainable progress in my relationship with God. The one thing I've discovered is God won't give you a vision that matches your bank account. I continue to have struggles just like everyone else, but I know where my help comes from. Surrendering my life to God has been the most epic experience I've ever had. I know God will continue to amaze me with the plans He has for my life, but I'll never feel worthy. It has nothing to do with low self-esteem, but in my deep reverence for Him.

Over the years, I have stopped worrying about what people think of me. I've learned how to enjoy the people who love and appreciate me just as I am, and not concern myself with those who don't. I've finally learned to embrace my perceived weaknesses, because they have become my strengths for the glory of God.

In spite of my checkered past living according to the world's way, God still has shown me favor. The Enemy's goal is to keep men divided and isolated so we can never realize and step into our true mission for our Lord and Savior Jesus Christ. As I stepped into my true purpose and calling, there were key lessons I had to learn:

- ▶ To be an effective witness for Christ, I had to free my mind of the world's way of thinking (Romans 12:2).
- ▶ I had to silence the noise of the world to hear the still, small voice of God (1 Kings 19:12).
- ▶ I learned to use my painful experiences with bullying and be a voice for the underdog; that is my mission (Matthew 25:40).
- ▶ Through my wholeness in Jesus Christ I've learned to embrace my brokenness (Colossians 2:9-10).
- ▶ I've learned to serve anyone whom I interact with as if I was serving God himself (Colossians 3:23).

The last major lesson I had to learn involved a stronghold keeping me from having a truly intimate relationship with God. That stronghold was tithing. Even before I accepted Jesus as my Savior in 2001, I had never agreed with tithing. I had allowed myself to become blinded by the Enemy and look at man and not God when it came to tithing.

In my immaturity, I refused to pay tithes because I didn't believe it was biblical for Christians today. I contended tithing was an Old Testament requirement. As such, up until February 2020, I wasn't a tither. However, that all changed after I fellowshipped with a Christian man whom I trust and respect. As we sat at a coffee shop, he informed me he had a burden on his heart to ask me something. I could sense he was reluctant to say it at first, but he finally asked me, "Are you a tither?" My reply was, "No, but my wife is." He then said, "But, you're the man. You're the covering over your home."

With all transparency, I felt a spiritual spear pierce my soul when he spoke the words, "But you're the man." In other words, "You can't hide behind your wife because that's not in line with God's command."

The last word he left me with was there's only one scripture in that Bible that allows us to test God. In Malachi 3, God tells man to test Him and trust Him with his tithe, and God would open up the windows of Heaven and pour out a blessing.

After our fellowship, I told him I would pray about it and do some research. Of course, I was only fooling myself at that point because I felt the peace of God come over me as he shared his heart with me. My fellowship with a true Christian man on that day was much needed and long overdue.

By the time I arrived home, I was convicted of disobeying God and looking at man. From that day forward in February 2020, I began tithing on everything I receive. I'm no longer bound by the Enemy's stronghold of deceit. I never could have imagined the blessings that have materialized since I began to trust God with my finances. I believe my reluctance to tithe was connected to my desire to control everything. This was another part of coming to the end of myself and releasing control of everything and totally trusting God. By sharing my tithing story, my intention is not to make you feel guilty if you're not paying tithes. I had to share the faithfulness and goodness of God of what my blessings have been as a result of tithing. The blessings of my tithing have gone far beyond my finances and have resulted in a freedom of transparency I've never had before. This was one of the main reasons why I was open to writing this book and sharing my testimony.

Conclusion

The mission of my book has been to share my life's testimony in the most transparent, open, and vulnerable way, to encourage other men from the age of eighteen to death to seek to become the men God intended you to be from your conception in the womb. I want men all over the world to believe, know, and understand it's okay to give place to and explore your emotions, in spite of the lie the world has taught us as men that sharing our feelings is a weakness. However, through my love and trust for Jesus Christ, I've learned transparency, vulnerability, and humility are actually strengths. These qualities have transformed me into the man God needs me to be in order to be an effective and efficient soldier for the Kingdom of God.

My mission is to enlighten and free as many men as I can by sharing the power of these qualities, because they enable you to be strong, powerful, and effective in all relationships. I want my story to be an encouragement for many boys and men to stop believing in the BIG LIE which says being emotional makes us less than a man. Being a soldier for Christ, I finally have peace and freedom in knowing that expressing myself emotionally doesn't make me less than a man; it makes me more of a man for the glory of God, and not for the approval of others.

Another reason I wrote this book was to explore the issue of abandonment—an unfortunate plague affecting a lot of men. It's never really discussed transparently, but such discussion is necessary for healing. I didn't begin to mature into a Christian/Kingdom man until I was 50 years old, because I was an angry boy who didn't have a Kingdom man teaching me how to be a man. One scripture in particular has helped me understand my growth into maturity as a soldier of Christ: *"When I was a child, I spoke as a child, I understood as a child, I thought as a child. But when I became a man, I put away childish things"* (1 Corinthians 13:11 NKJV).

I went from being an angry boy to a prideful and stubborn male who masqueraded as a man. My anger was birthed by the bullying I endured from first grade through high school. I was bullied because I was shy and didn't have the courage or confidence to speak up for myself and very few people came to my defense during that period of my life. My book has ultimately been about me going from being bullied, to bullying, to becoming a servant soldier for Jesus Christ, because of a praying grandmother, mother, and wife.

In the end, I finally learned to love Damon Jones, forgiven son of my Lord and Savior Jesus Christ. I had to embrace and accept the person I saw in the mirror every day.

I accept myself for who I am and WHOSE I am, in spite of what the world tells me.

"You are of God, little children, and have overcome them, because He who is in you is greater than he who is in the world." (1 John 4:4 NKJV)

For Speaking Engagements, Book Signings,
Appearances, and Interviews...

CONTACT

info@purposevideoservices.com

562-688-6279

www.PurposeVideoServices.com

www.DroneFilmEdit101.com